WINDOWS 10

USER'S GUIDE

Get Everything You Need to Know About 2019 Windows 10 Home and Professional Update

CHARLES
SMITH

Copyright

All rights reserved. No part of this publication **Windows 10 User Guide** may be reproduced, stored in a retrieval system or transmitted in any form or by any means - electronic, mechanical, photocopying, recording, and scanning without permission in writing by the author.

Printed in the United States of America
© 2019 by Charles Smith

Churchgate Publishing House

USA | UK | Canada

Table of Contents

Copyright i
Why This Guide? vi
About the Author vii
Introduction to Windows 10 1
Windows 10 Home or Windows 10 Pro Which Should I Get? 2
Start Menu 7
How to Add Applications to the Tiles Section 9
Accessing the Start Menu Options 11
How to Pin Apps to the Task Bar 12
Task View 16
Using the Search Tool 16
Setting up Cortana 17
Some Funny Questions to Ask Cortana 20
Cortana Shortcuts 20
Using Edge Browser 20
Microsoft Store 23
Settings And Control Panel 23
Customizing the Look and Feel of Windows 10 Desktop . 25
Connecting to a Projector and Using Extended Desktop . 27
Activating Tablet Mode 28
How to use the snap feature 29

Using the Snipping Tool	29
Changing Default Printer	31
Windows Updates and Defender	31
Installing Apps Using Ninite	33
Useful Apps to Install on Windows 10	34
How to Uninstalling Apps	37
File Explorer	38
File Manager	40
Customizing Privacy Settings	45
Network and Internet Settings	51
How to Lock Your Computer	53
How to Install Windows 10 on MacBook Pro	53
New Features and Capabilities of Windows 10 version 1903	57
Windows Mixed Reality	66
Windows Sandbox	66
Narrator	68
Windows Settings	70
Other Tips and Tricks	73
Dark Themes	73
Game Mode	73
Storage Sense	74
Night Light	74

Shop with Edge 74
Print to PDF 75
Virtual Desktops 75
Emoji 75
God Mode 76
Useful Hot Key Combinations for Windows 10 76
Shutting Down your Computer 78
Troubleshooting Problems 79
Keyboard Not Working 79
Troubleshoot blue Screen 80
Troubleshoot Memory Leak 80
Troubleshooting Start up issues 84
Wi-Fi Not Connecting 90
Troubleshooting Wi-Fi disconnecting frequently 93
Remote Desktop Connection not Working 95
Mail App Not Working 99
Complete Clean, format or reinstall Windows 10 100
Speed up Windows 10 103
Final Note 108

Why This Guide?

Whether you are new to Windows 10 having just upgraded from an older Operating System or you have recently purchased a new Personal Computer with Windows 10 Operating System pre-installed or like many others you have migrated from the MacOS from Apple and have finally made a switch to Windows computer or you are in need of tips and tricks to enable you master the Windows 10 Operating System and troubleshoot common problems, then this guide is for you.

To get you started, we will look at some basic to advanced settings on Windows 10, perform a specific task with Windows, dig deeper into the settings menu, take advantage of Cortana, look at the new features of the 2019 Windows 10 update and take an extensive tour of Window 10 Operating System. The book also contains tips to hidden advanced features for the Windows 10 you may never find anywhere.

About the Author

Charles Smith is a tech enthusiast with over 13 years experience in the ICT industry. He is a geek and passionately follows the latest technical and technological trends. His strength lies in figuring out the solution to complex tech problems. Charles holds a Bachelor and a Master's Degree in Computer Science and Information Communication Technology respectively from the MIT, Boston Massachusetts.

Introduction to Windows 10

Insert a sharper version

Windows 10 is a personal computer operating system developed and released by Microsoft. Windows 10 operating system was released on the 29th of July 2015 and was considered one of the best operating systems to date. Windows 10 operating system is platform independent, that is, it works on different platforms - laptops, desktops, tablets, smartphones, Xbox etc. Another reason why Windows 10 is considered the best operating system is the release of continuous updates by Microsoft to improve the user's experience. Additionally, Windows 10 has a much faster boot up time. It also offers the tablet-to-PC mode, voice-activated commands using Cortana, enhanced search and so on.

Windows 10 Home or Windows 10 Pro Which Should I Get?

If you purchased a PC with Windows 10 pre-installed, it is most likely it came with the Windows 10 Home. You may be wondering what the difference between these different Windows 10 versions is and which is best for you. There is no much difference between windows 10 pro and the Home version. First of all, let's look at the Windows 10 Home; this edition costs $119 and it has one hundred percent Windows feature any regular user will need, especially if they are not professionals.

The only real "limitation" with Windows 10 Home edition is the amount of Random Access Memory (RAM) it requires, which is a whopping 128GB. This is less than what is required by Windows 10 Pro. Another noticeable difference is the absence of BitLocker in Windows 10 Home, which is present in Windows 10 Pro. BitLocker is a security feature that allows users to encrypt the entire hard drive in a PC. Which means a password is required to boot up the PC. What this does is, even if someone takes out the hard drive from the PC, they still won't be able to access your data.

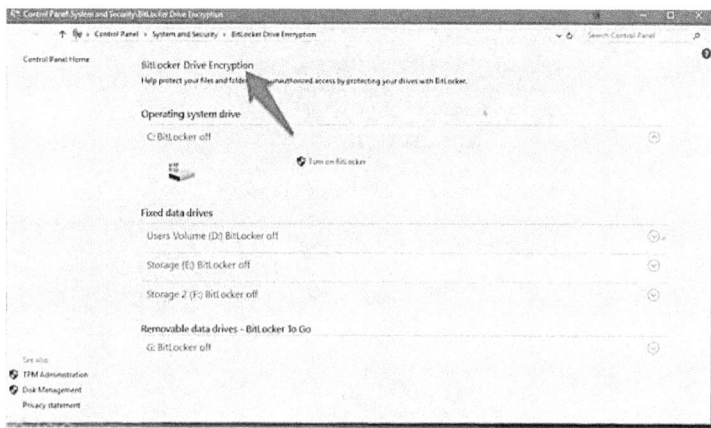

The Windows 10 Pro comes at $199, which is $80 more than Windows 10 Home edition. It has the Hyper-V feature which allows native support for running virtual computers on Windows. However, this feature can be performed by third-party software like Virtual box on Windows 10 Home. It will enable users to run multiple instances of Windows or other operating system and have them isolated from the default operating system. These virtual operating systems could be used for testing, developing or security purpose (for instance, you may need to test software, but you are not sure it is safe to do so without affecting your operating system). The next feature, Windows 10 Pro offers is the Remote Desktop. All versions of Windows supports remote desktop in the sense that you can control other devices (laptop, desktop, tablets) remotely from a PC running Windows 10 Pro. However, only a PC running Windows 10 Pro or higher editions can control other PCs running Windows 10 Pro, in other words, a PC running Windows 10 Home cannot control another PC running Windows 10 Pro.

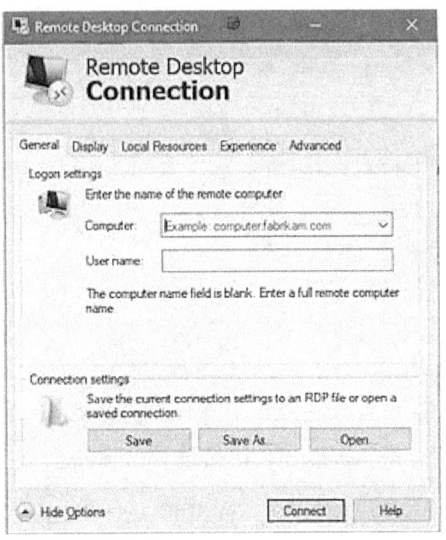

However, there are still third-party software that allows you to do this if you don't have a Windows 10 Pro. Another exciting feature of the Windows 10 Pro is the ability to delay updates. Windows 10 Home does not allow users to delay updates whenever they are available, but Windows 10 Pro will enable you to postpone the update for up to a month or more especially the enterprise edition which allows you to delay updates indefinitely. Having said this, it is not advisable to disable window's update altogether. You always want to keep Windows up-to-date for security reasons. But if you are a professional who uses Windows, then it could be helpful to delay updates in case you are worried about the update breaking something that is work-critical. This could be especially so for the major updates they do twice in a year like the "Microsoft creators update" which do break a lot of stuff.

The other features may not be useful to everyone except in a business environment, for instance - "Domain Join". With "Domain Join", you could use the Windows 10 Pro version to connect to a domain which allows your computer to be controlled by an admin and other PCs in that network. Relatively, the Windows 10 Pro has the "Group Policy Editor" which allows Admins to mass control configurations on different computers in a network.

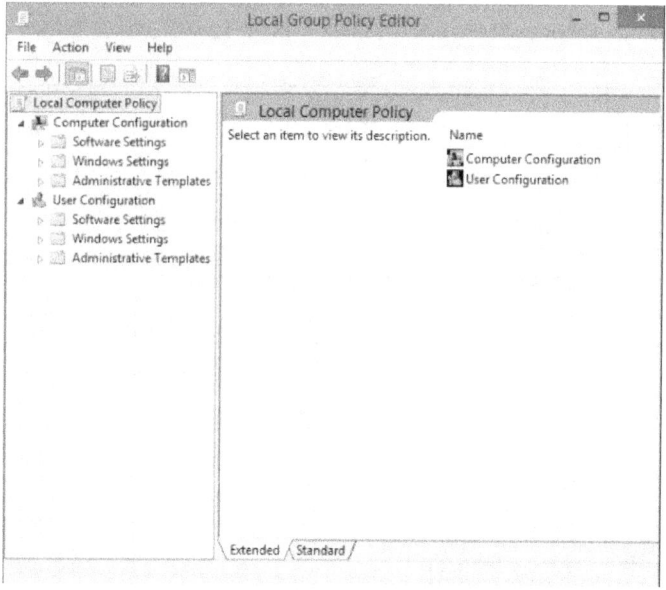

Another exciting feature of the Pro version is the "Assigned Access," which allows a user to restrict the computer or another user from been able to use anything on the PC except for a particular app. E.g., A Salesperson with access only to a Point-of-Sales App on a PC in a Shopping Mall.

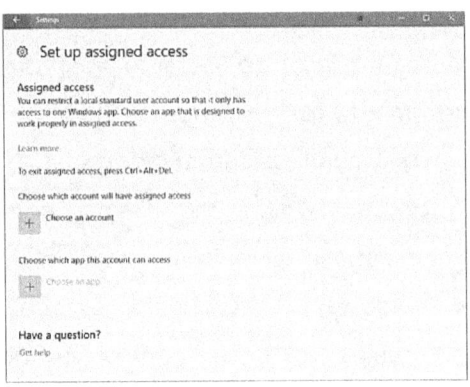

Finally, the Windows 10 Pro version, has a feature called "Windows Store for Business," which allows users to purchase volume app licenses. For instance, if you have up to ten business computers, you can buy an app with different licenses and install it easily to all ten computers without having to purchase ten apps for each computer.

There are other Windows 10 versions worth mentioning to give you an idea of what they do. They are Windows 10 Enterprise, Education, IoT and Windows 10S. Windows 10 Enterprise is designed to be deployed on several computers in a large organization that has many computers. It allows for volume licensing and direct control from one central admin.

Windows 10 Education version is similar to enterprise except that it is focused on institutions of learning (e.g. University, Colleges, etc). However, unlike the Enterprise Edition, Windows 10 Education focuses on Academic volume licensing instead of corporate.

Another not so popular version of Windows is the Windows IoT Core. It is meant for Internet of Things devices. It is a very basic version of Windows 10 that runs on devices like Raspberry pie and other low powered devices that require an Operating System.

There is also the Newer Windows 10S which is a knocked down version of Windows 10. It allows the user only to run Window's Store Apps.

Start Menu

The start button is the window icon ■ at the lower left corner of the taskbar. The start menu is redesigned in Windows 10. It is a combination of Windows 7 menu and tiles on the right side, which is prevalent in Windows 8.

On the start menu, the most used applications are placed at the upper left part, as shown below.

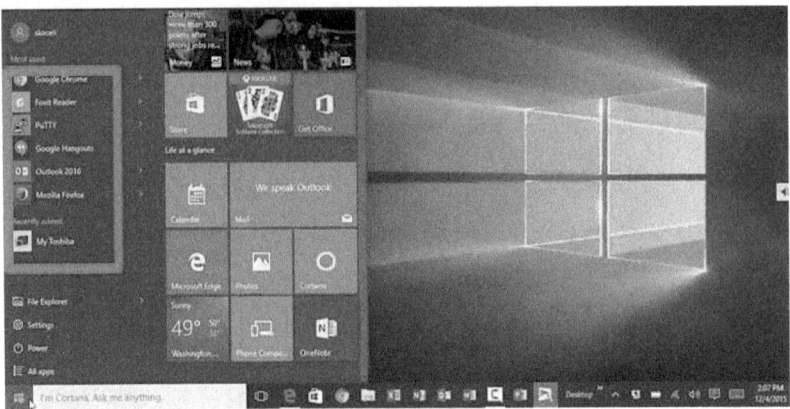

At the lower left part of the Start Menu, is the File Explorer, settings, power options and All Apps. The "All Apps" has the same features as "All Programs" in Windows 7.

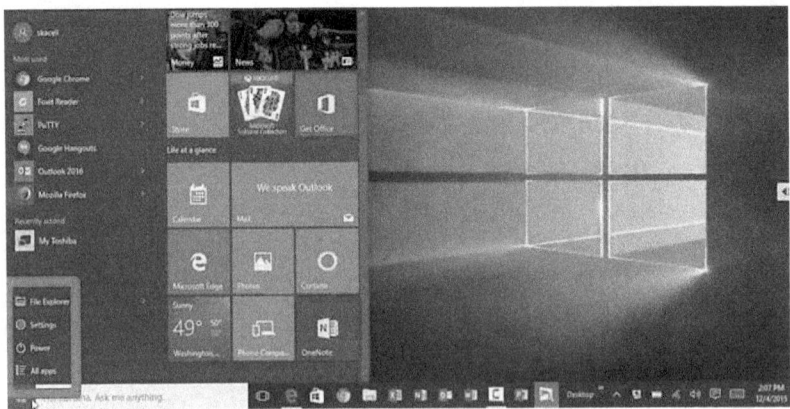

The tiles are displayed on the right side of the menu, as shown in the screenshot below. The tiles are squares with various functionality.

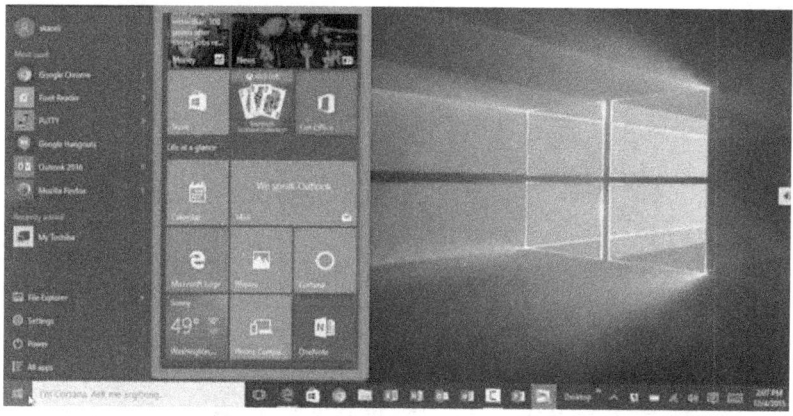

How to Add Applications to the Tiles Section

To add an application to the tiles section - Click on the "Start" menu - Click on "All Apps."

9

Scroll down and pick whichever apps you want - right-click on the app - Click on "Pin to start". This action moves the App to the tiles section. Do it for as much app you wish to move to the tiles section.

You can also place and name the recently added apps in a group. To do this, hover your mouse pointer at the top of the newly added apps until you see the "Name group." Click on the "Name group" and type in any name you wish to give to the group of recently added apps. You can also move the group by clicking and dragging it to whichever part of the tile section you wish to move them to.

Accessing the Start Menu Options

If you right-click on the "Start icon " ⊞ (you will be presented with several options for easy access. To customize the start menu, click on the start menu - "Settings" - "Personalization."

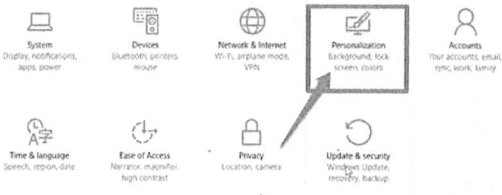

Under "personalization," there are several options you can customize. For instance, Background, colors, lock screen, themes and the Start Menu. Click on "Start" to allow you customize additional options on the start menu by either enabling or disabling the different options. Some of the features that can be customized include "Show more tiles," "occasionally show suggestions in start", "show most used apps", "show recently added apps," "Use Start full screen" or "show recently opened items in jump lists on start or the taskbar".

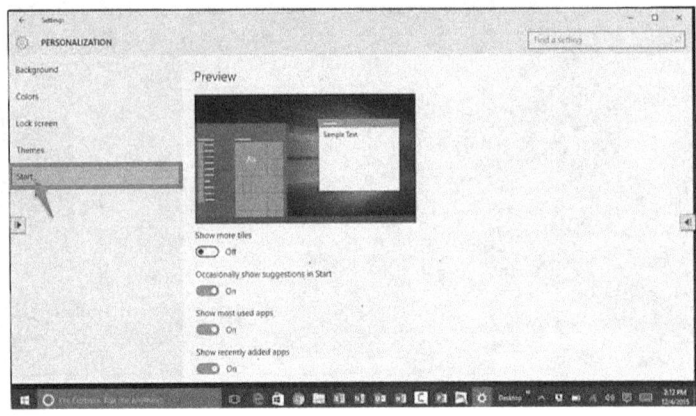

How to Pin Apps to the Task Bar

The taskbar, like in previous versions of windows holds the start menu, the search box, pinned applications and on the extreme right side, the controls. You can pin any application you need quick access to, on the task bar. To do this, click "Start" ■ - "All Apps" - scroll down to the App you wish to pin on the taskbar and right-click on the App - click on "More" - "Pin to taskbar."

The app is then pinned to the taskbar. Alternatively, you can right-click on the app in the tile section - click on "More" - "Pin to taskbar". If you no longer need an app on the taskbar, right-click on the app and left-click on "unpin it from the taskbar". One of the additions to the taskbar in Windows 10 is the "Action Center."

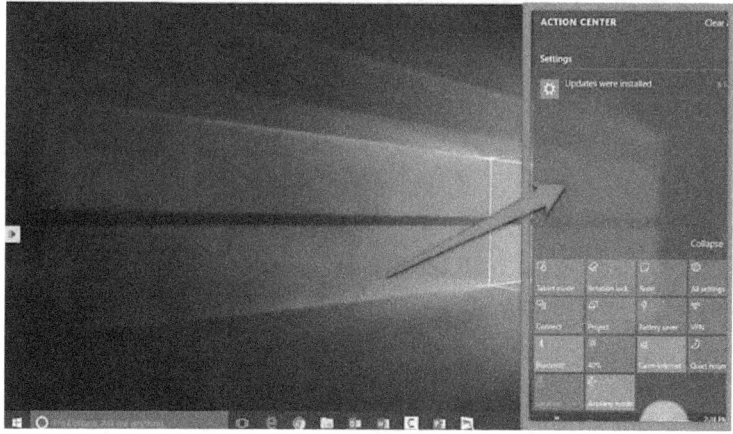

The action center displays activities on the computer that requires attention. To customize the action center, right-click on the right end of the taskbar - click on any of the different options that are listed to either show or hide it, for instance, "show or hide" task view button, show or hide touch keyboard button etc. If you do not have a touch screen, it will be unnecessary to display the touch keyboard button. Customizing the action center also gives you options to configure Cortana (which we will cover in a moment), show windows side by side, show windows stacked etc.

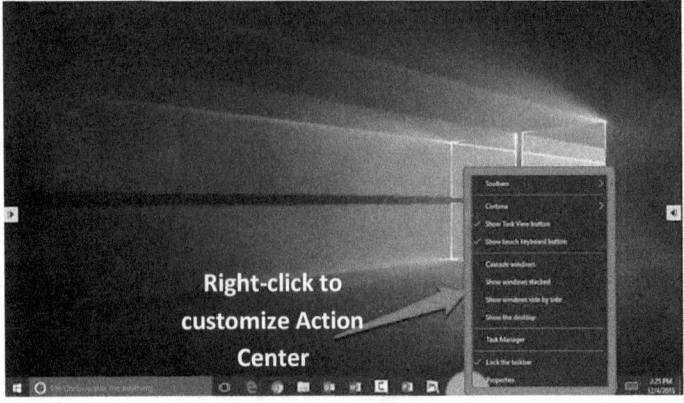

One other option we need to consider is under "Property." Under the "Taskbar and Start Properties," you can either lock the taskbar, auto-hide the taskbar or reduce the size of icons on the taskbar. Additionally, you can change the position you wish to place the taskbar (bottom, left, right or top), you can also customize what shows up on the "notification area" on the "Taskbar and start menu properties" dialogue box. To do this, right-click on the "notification area" of the taskbar - scroll down and click on "properties" - on the "taskbar and start menu" properties dialogue box, click on "Customize" next to "Notification area."

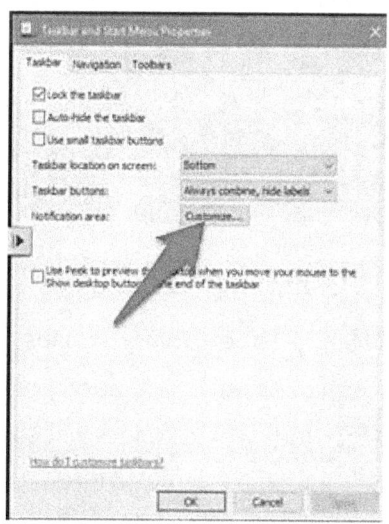

Here you have several options on what you want to be displayed on the "notification area" under "Notification & Actions." You can turn ON or OFF any of the notifications options listed.

Task View

The "task view" option is a new feature in Windows 10. This is similar to the "Alt-Tab" option of previous Windows operating system. However, it allows you to move between several open applications and switch to the App you wish to make the active screen. To do this, press "Alt + Tab" on the keyboard or click on the task view button on the task bar as shown in the screenshot below.

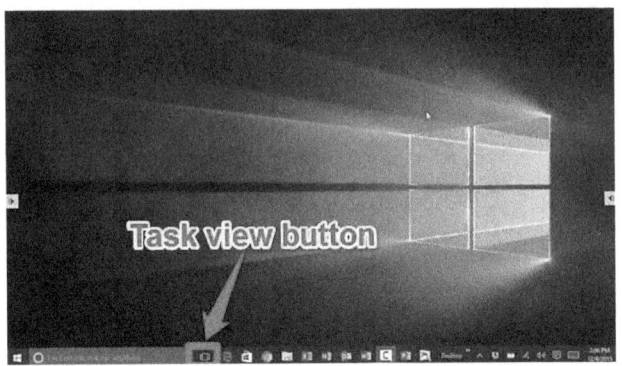

Using the Search Tool

The search tool as the name implies enables you to search for applications, files, folders, settings, etc in the computer. The search tool was available in Windows 7 and 8, but an improved introduced in Windows 10 Operating System. To use the search tool, left-click on the start icon then type the file, app, or settings you wish to find in the search box. It locates the application, settings or file even before you are done typing the name and you can click on it to open.

Notice that as you use the search capabilities there is an option to the left to configure it. You can from this option specify whether to turn Cortana ON/OFF, clear search history or limit your search to the operating system or extend it to the web. It also provides options to set up additional privacy and search engine results.

Setting up Cortana

Cortana performs a content-based search on your PC and other devices that supports it. With Cortana, you can send text messages, identify a song, pause and play music as well as change settings in windows 10 using voice command. However, Cortana is designed for US residents only; but you can still use Cortana even if you are not resident in the United States. Here are the steps to take to activate Cortana as a non-US resident - In the search bar, type "Region & Language" - scroll down and select "United States." Close the "Region & Language" menu.

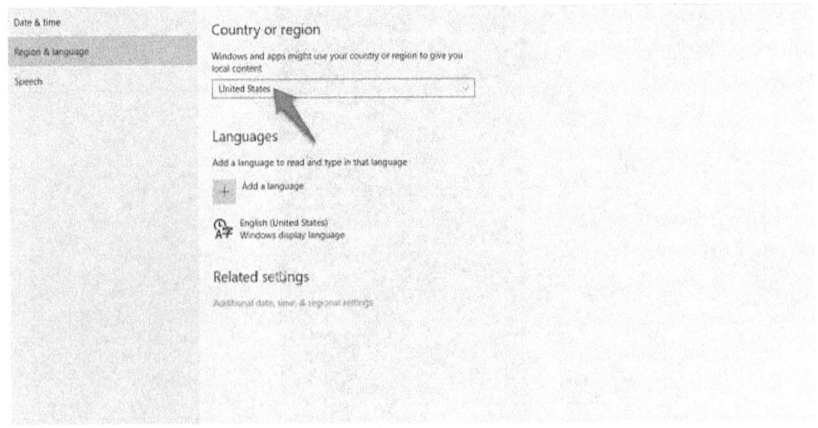

Open "Settings" menu and turn ON Cortana.

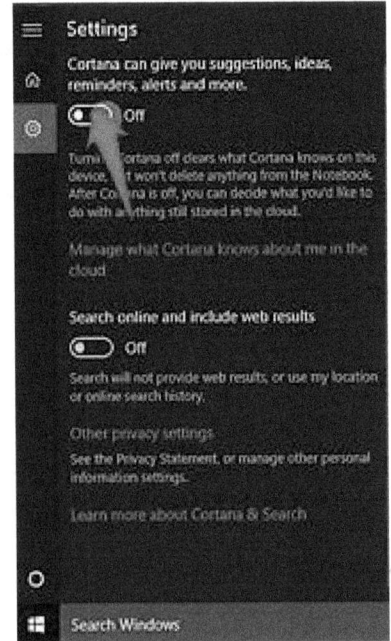

Agree to the Privacy statement for using Cortana

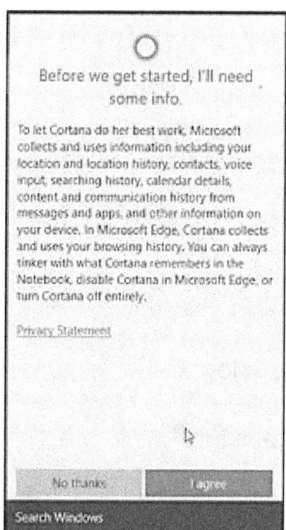

With Cortana activated, you can start asking it questions. You can also train your Cortana to recognize your voice alone. To do this, type "Cortana Settings" in the search box –click the "To me" radio button beneath "Respond best."

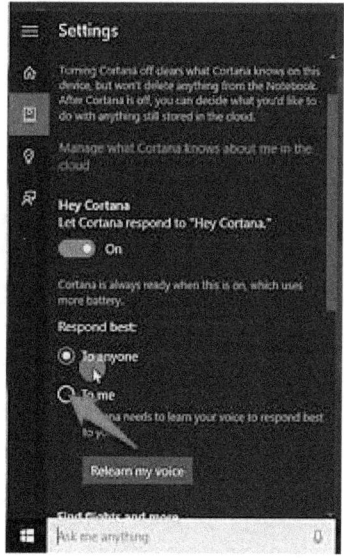

Some Funny Questions to Ask Cortana

Hey Cortana, Who is your Father?

Hey Cortana, Can I see you?

Hey Cortana, What do you think about Google?

Hey Cortana, Are you Male or Female?

Hey Cortana, do you know me?

Hey Cortana, Are you lying?

Hey Cortana, what do you think of bing?

Other questions to ask Cortana are:

Hey Cortana, open Google Chrome?

Hey Cortana, what's the weather today?

Hey Cortana, turn OFF Bluetooth.

Hey Cortana, convert $3281 to £

Cortana Shortcuts

Windows Key ⊞ + Q = Opens the Cortana Home Screen

Windows Key ⊞ + S = Allow you type into Cortana

Windows Key ⊞ + C = Send Cortana into listening Mode

Using Edge Browser

Microsoft Edge enables users to surf the internet on Windows 10. However, you can download and install other browsers like Safari, Google Chrome, Firefox, etc. = browsers Here, we will be looking at some features that are available in Microsoft Edge. Click on Microsoft Edge from the taskbar.

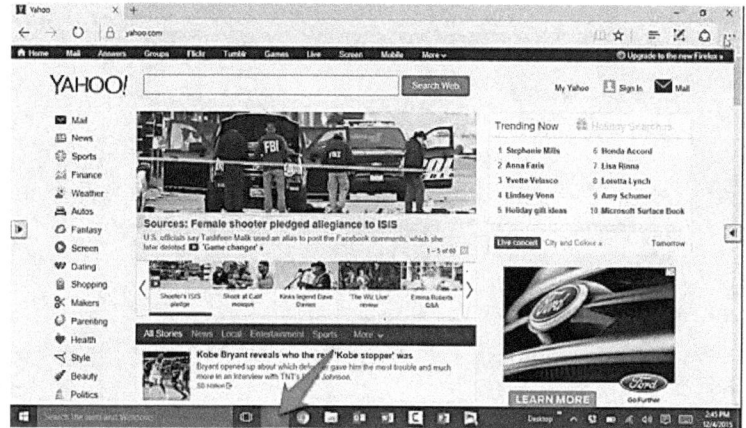

The address bar is at the top of the page. Next to the address bar, you have the browser options button.

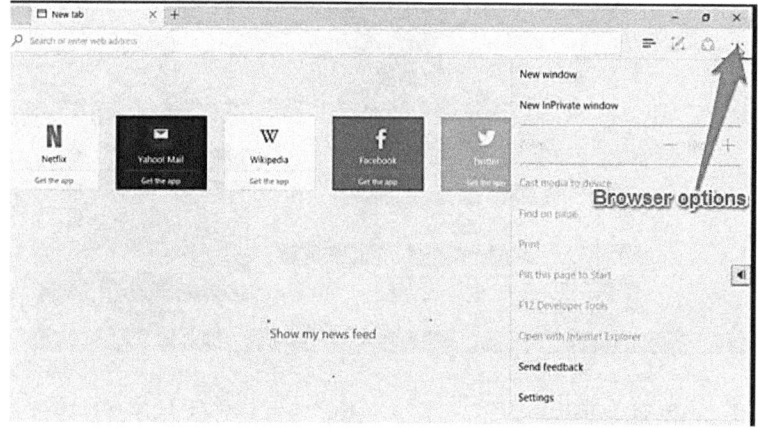

One of the features of Microsoft edge browser over other browsers is the ability to annotate on the screen. To do this, click on the "Web note" icon to have access to annotation tools.

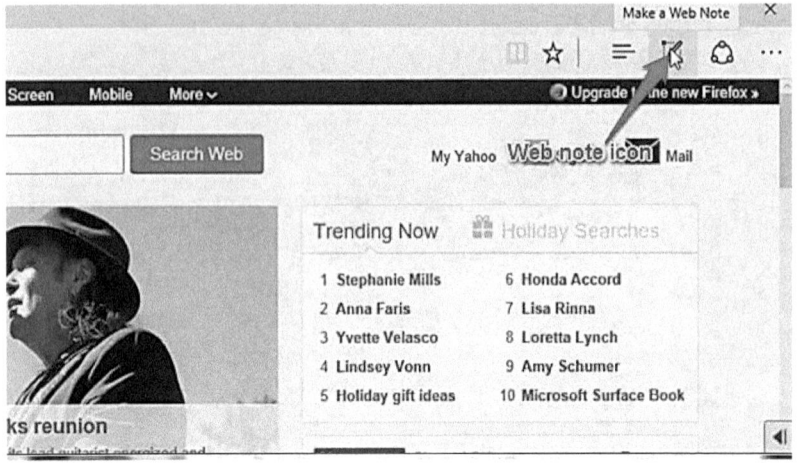

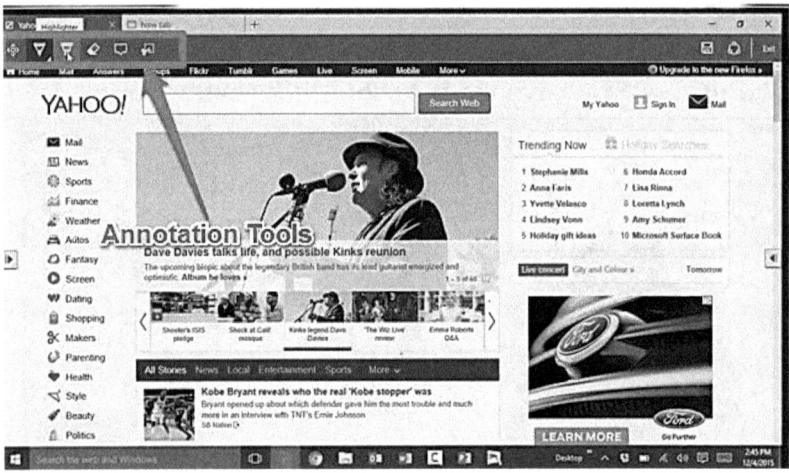

With the annotation tools, you can pick colors to annotate or highlight certain areas directly on the webpage if for instance you are doing a presentation or doing a demo for teaching and you wish to highlight or annotate specific area on the webpage to buttress your point. Other things you can

22

do with the annotation option include - using the eraser tool to clear annotations and highlights, save web notes for future reference by clicking the save icon 🖫 etc. When you are done with the annotation tool, click on the exit button at the top right.

Microsoft Store

One of the things you get from installing the Windows 10 Operating System is the ability to download Apps from Microsoft Store in a way similar to Google Playstore or the Apple Store. To download an app from the store, click on start - in the search box, type in the "Store," left-click on "store" to open the trusted Window Store 🖫. In the store, search for apps, games, music, movies and TV series to download.

Settings And Control Panel

One of the latest features of the Windows 10 Operating system is the consolidated settings. Unlike in Windows 8, where settings options are scattered all over the place, in

Windows 10, all the settings are under "Settings Menu." To get to the settings menu, click on "Start" - "Settings". One of the advantages of the Windows 10 settings panel is the ability to search for whatever settings you want. For instance, if you don't know where to get the "password settings," you can simply type "Password" in the search bar and you will find everything that has to do with changing password.

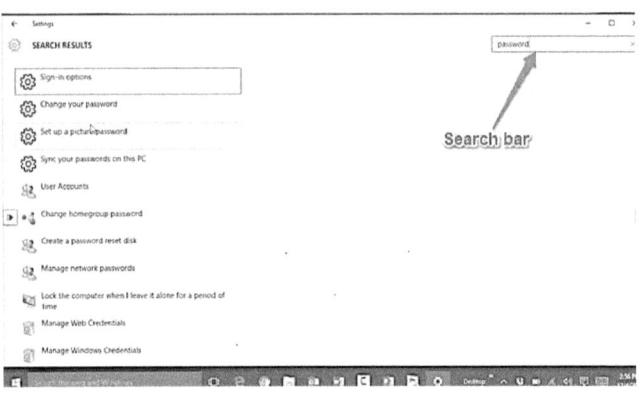

The search can also be performed in the search box at the desktop. To access the control panel on Windows 10, right click on "Start" and left-click on the Control Panel. This will give you a similar view as in window 7 and 8.

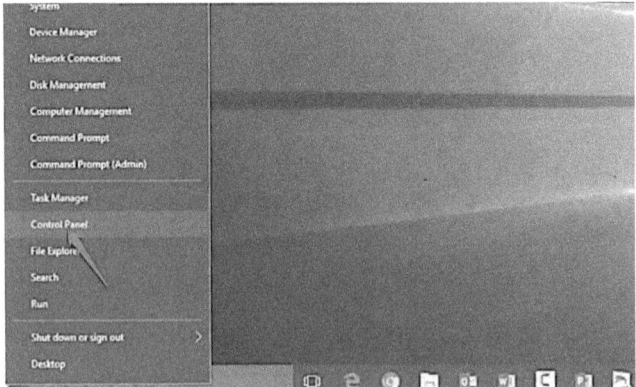

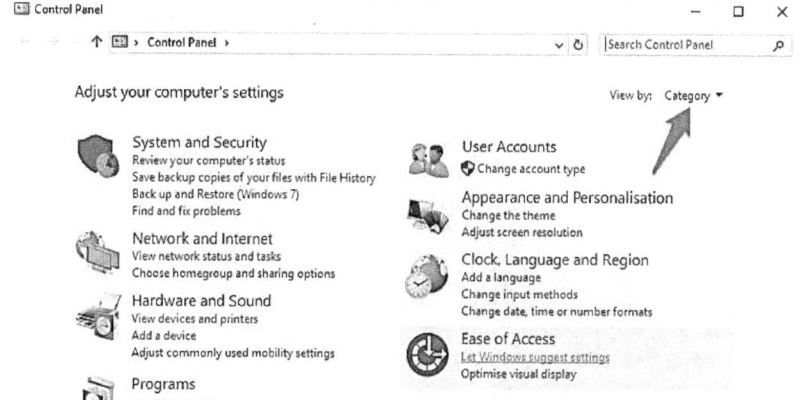

To change the arrangement of icons in the control panel, click on "Category" next to "View by" at the top-right side of the control panel window. The icons can be set to either large or small, depending on the user's preference. You can also use the search box within the control panel window to search for any control panel-related settings.

Customizing the Look and Feel of Windows 10 Desktop

Various customizations can be done on the desktop of Windows 10 and there are also a couple of ways to go about it. One of these is to right-click on the desktop and click on "Personalize." This will open up a "Personalization" Window where you can carry out different customizations.

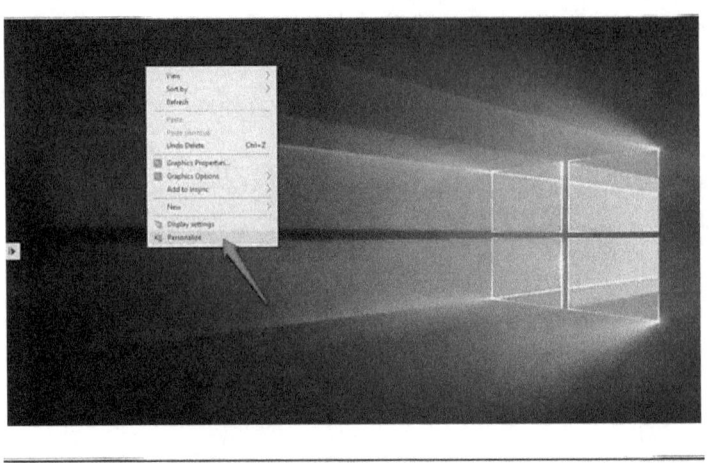

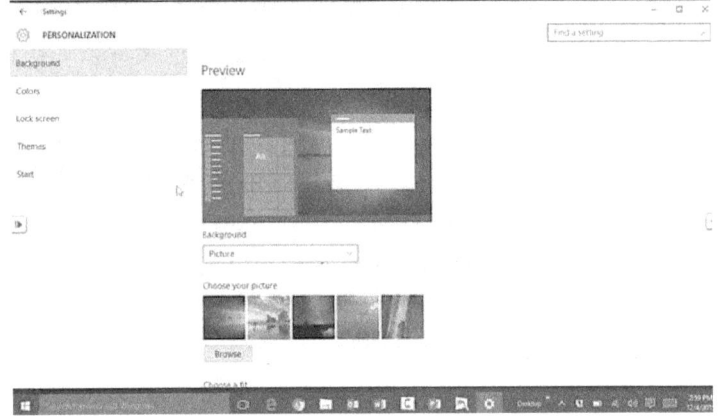

From the personalization menu, you can select options to customize the desktop background, color, lock screen, theme and start menu. Users can also choose pictures for the background different from the default image. This option also changes the theme and colors to match the selected background image. You can choose to "fit" the image on the entire desktop. For the colors, you can choose to pick an accent color from your background automatically. You can also turn OFF this feature if you don't like it. There are other exciting customization options such as "show color on start, action center and title bar - Make start, taskbar and action center transparent - high contrast settings and so on.

For the "Lock Screen", you can choose the lock screen image. You can also select "windows spotlight action" or "slide show" for the lock screen. Another Personalization option is desktop theme customization - Click on "Theme settings" under themes - under theme settings - change themes, get more themes online, change the color you want to be applied to a theme, change desktop icons and mouse pointer.

You can also hide shortcut icons and folders on the desktop on your computer by simply right-clicking on the desktop - Click on "View" - "Hide desktop icons". To unhide desktop icons, follow the same steps and click on "unhide desktop icons."

Connecting to a Projector and Using Extended Desktop

In this section, we will be looking at how to connect your laptop to a projector or a second display screen. This feature has been around in previous windows as well, but there is a slight difference in where it is located in Windows 10. There are several ways to connect your laptop to a projector or a second display monitor and one of the ways to do this is through the "Actionv Center". Right-click on the notification area on the taskbar and select "Project".

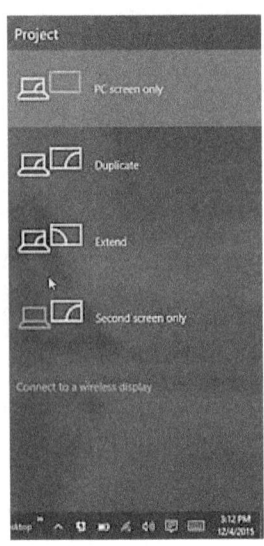

If you wish to display a presentation on a projector, click on "Duplicate". Click on "Extend" if you have two monitors connected to your PC. This is ideal for a laptop or desktop that has two video inputs. With this, you can simultaneously open different apps on the two monitors. You can also move the mouse from monitor 1 to monitor 2 back and forth. The second option used in accessing the project menu is press on the window key and "P" on the keyboard.

Activating Tablet Mode

Windows 10 is designed for desktop, tablets and mobile devices. If you have a laptop that can be converted to a tablet by simply detaching the keyboard, you can change the mode from regular PC mode to a tablet mode. One of the ways to do this is to go to the "Action Center" - click on "Tablet mode". Note that when tablet mode is activated, you are expected to use the touch screen to open and navigate through the device. You can also use various swipe actions to navigate through the tablet. Left swipe gives you access to the task view, swiping from top to bottom will close an existing application and tapping on the right side of the window to reveal the "Action Center." To switch back to PC mode, go back to the "Action Mode" and uncheck the "tablet mode."

How to use the snap feature

The snap feature has been around in Windows 7, 8 and now Windows 10. When an App window is open, pressing the windows key and the Left arrow on the keyboard will resize the App window to the left. If you choose to resize and move a specific window to the right, press the Windows key and the right arrow on the keyboard. This way, you can open two apps or programs and work on them simultaneously.

Using the Snipping Tool

The snipping tool has been around since Windows 7, but it is handy in Windows 10 Operating System. To use the snipping tool, press the Windows key and search for the Snipping tool in the search box.

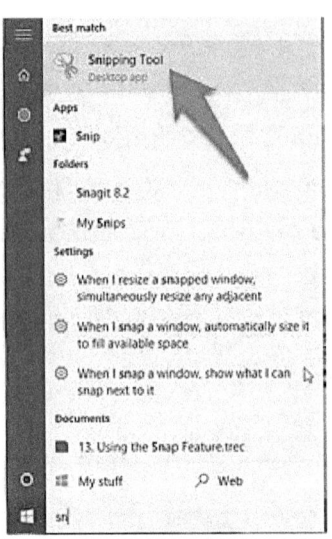

Click on it to open the Snipping tool menu

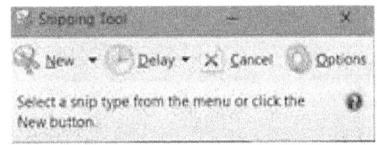

What the snipping tool does is that it enables users to take a screenshot of the entire desktop or a portion of the desktop to be part of a document or mail. To do this, open the snipping tool menu - click on "New" - Drag the mouse cursor around any portion of the screen you wish to capture - you can add highlights, annotation or use the pencil or eraser tool on the captured screen - then click on the "Save" icon to save the snip. You can as well copy it and paste in a document or an email.

Changing Default Printer

Users can change the default printer settings to accommodate an available printer. Click on the "window key" - in the search bar, type "printer" - click on "Devices and Printers" - Connect your printer to the laptop or desktop - the new printer icon will appear on the lists of connected printers - right-click on the printer you wish to set as default - Click on "Set as default printer". A green check mark appears by the side of the selected printer indicating it is now the default printer.

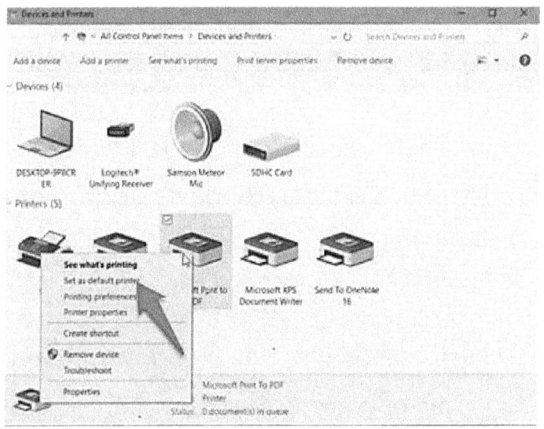

This becomes the first choice of printer the PC sends files to whenever you wish to print a document or photo.

Windows Updates and Defender

Although Microsoft regularly updates the Windows 10 Operating System, it is important to check if new updates are available. There are a couple of ways to get to Windows update on Windows 10. You could either click on "Start" - "Settings" - "update & Security" or simply press the windows key on the keyboard and in the search bar type in "Check for updates". At this point, if there is an update waiting for you to install, click on the "Install Now" button.

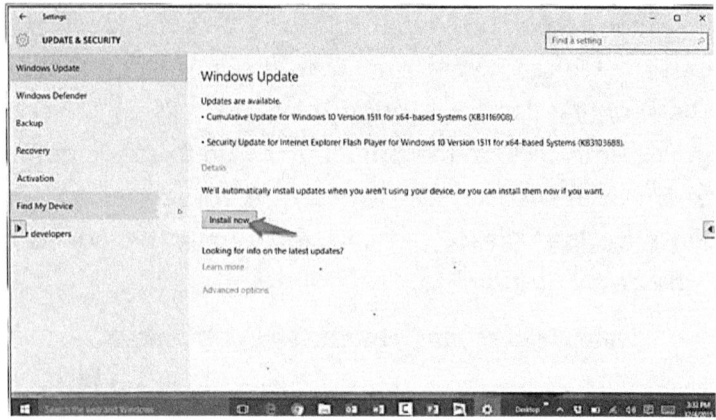

Note that sometimes, the updates take a little longer to finish installing. It is ideal to perform Windows Update at periods you wouldn't need your computer for at least 20 minutes or more.

Windows 10 also comes with the Windows Defender. If you are not using any other antivirus, you can schedule system scans for virus and Malware from time to time with Windows Defender - type "Windows Defender" in the search box to access the program. Users can either perform a quick scan, full scan or custom scan (scheduled scan). You can also carry out a manual update of the Windows Defender by clicking on "Update". You can change and tweak additional settings on the Windows Defender by clicking on "Settings" at the top right corner.

Installing Apps Using Ninite

Ninite is not part of the Windows 10 operating system, but it is a great way to install Windows applications. Click on the Edge browser on the taskbar or type Edge browser in the search box - in the URL type ninite.com.

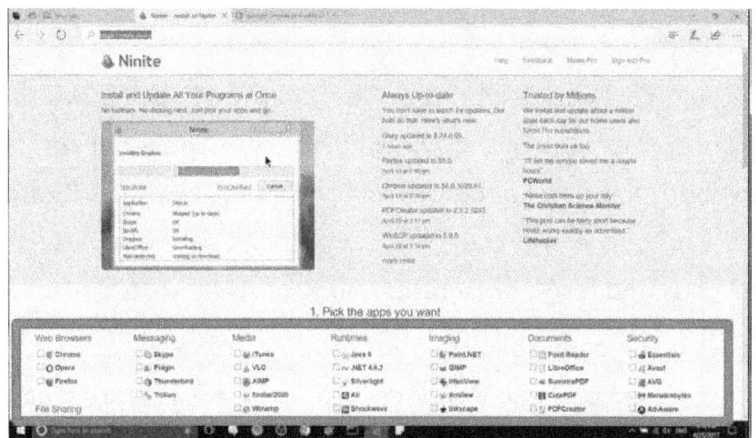

On the ninite web page, choose the apps you want installed on your PC by left-clicking in the checkboxes. When you are done selecting apps, click on "Get You Ninite" to download and install all the selected apps in your computer.

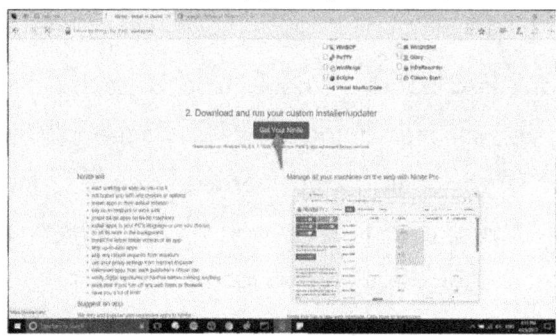

33

Useful Apps to Install on Windows 10

In this section, we will be looking at some useful apps that you may find handy on your PC. These apps are all available in the stores.

QuickLook App: This app enables a quick preview of files by just hitting the space bar.

Ueli Search App: Ueli brings a launcher to windows, which is similar to the spotlight on Mac. Press "Alt + Spacebar" on the keyboard to open up the Ueli launcher to quickly launch apps, files and online searches. You can customize the look of the launcher and also create custom shortcuts.

Groupy: Groupy allows users to use several apps and software on a single window in a browser-like tab style. If you are worried that multiple tabs will ruin things up, don't worry, groupy groups tabs from a single app like the browsers into a single collection. Groupy also has a range of customization options users can take advantage of. This app is available for a 30-day free trial after which users will pay $5 for the full version.

Franz: Franz is a handy Window app because it allows you to access all your messaging apps like Facebook Messenger, Whatsapp, Skype, email, and more on your PC in a unified interface. All you need to do is add the services you use from a list of messenger apps on the app window.

ShareX: ShareX is a screenshot app packed with useful features. With ShareX you can take different types of screenshots, for instance, the screenshot of a section, screenshot of an app window, or even set things to auto capture. You can set the ShareX to automatically save the screenshots or upload it to a host like Google photos.

PeaZip: PeaZip is a free compression tool which allows you to open almost all types of compression file formats. It also lets you create achieves in different formats. PeaZip does not only allow you to create encrypted achieves, but it also allows you to create file achieves with two-factor authentication. Apart from this, it has all the features you can expect from a compression tool like the ability to split and join achieves, built-in file managers, secure deleting of files and so on.

WizTree: If you own a laptop with 128GB or 256GB hard disk, you must have faced low storage issues and you may not know what is taking up most of the storage space. With WizTree, a free app, you can search for the files and folders using up the most disk space on your device. Open the WizTree App - select the drive and click on Scan. After the scan is complete, WizTree shows you a visual map of your files so you can spot the large files with ease.

Converter Bot: This is a handy free tool in Windows 10 if you convert files a lot. It is an app that supports more than 300 file types so you can preview any file you want and convert them to any file type. For instance, if you have a PDF file, you can load it up into the Converter Bot and view it or convert it to another file type.

EarTrumpet: This is a powerful volume control app available for free in the Windows Store. It provides users with the ability to control volumes of individual apps. With EarTrumpet, you could set say music to play on the external speakers while the sound from a game plays on an earphone.

Multiswipe: Windows 10 has support for a few multi-touch gestures, but you can add more with Multiswipe. Multiswipe allows users to create custom two-fingers, three-fingers or even four-finger gestures with the touchpad and the touch screen. For instance, you can create two-finger swipe up and down on the touchpad or screen to increase or decrease volume. You could also set two-tap gestures to switch between tabs in the browser quickly. Multiswipe is available for a free trial of fifteen days after which you will need to get the full version for $5.

How to Uninstalling Apps

To uninstall an app on Windows 10, click on the start icon on the taskbar - in the search box, type "Add or remove programs."

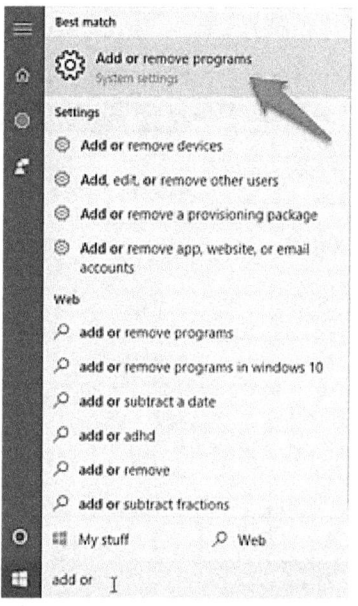

This will list all the installed Apps on your PC - scroll to the App you wish to uninstall and right-click on it - Click on "Uninstall," and this will remove the App from your computer. It may be helpful when you purchase a new PC with a preinstalled Windows 10 and you wish to uninstall the unnecessary apps that came along. If you want to access the old Add/Remove program window - type appwiz.cpl in the search box and hit the enter button on the keyboard.

File Explorer

A File Explorer is a tool used for accessing all files on the hard drive. Generally, most PCs have one drive known as Local Disk (C). There are several ways to access File Explorer. Click on "Start" - left-click on "File Explorer" or you can click on File Explorer directly on the taskbar.

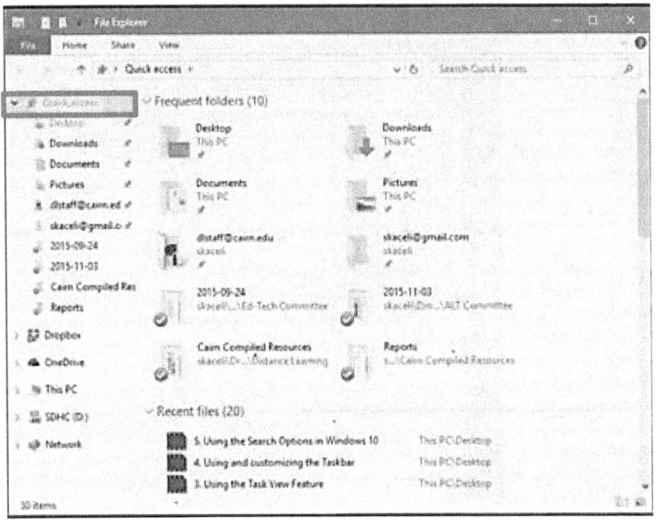

When you access the File Explorer window, a new addition to note is the "Quick Access". "Quick Access" gives users access to recent and frequently used files and folders. These recent files and folders are listed at the left-hand side. You can add a file to the "Quick Access" menu by right-clicking on them and "Pin to Quick Access". You can as well unpin it from the "Quick Access" menu by right-clicking on the file, and then click on "Unpin from Quick Access".

You can also change the way folders are displayed on the file explorer - While in "File Explorer - Click on "View" - you will see different display settings you can customize your folders to under "view," e.g., small icons, large icons, details, extra large icons, medium icons and list. Whatever view option you select applies to the particular folder you are viewing. If you want it applied to all folders in the computer - Click on "View" - "Options" - "change folder and search options".

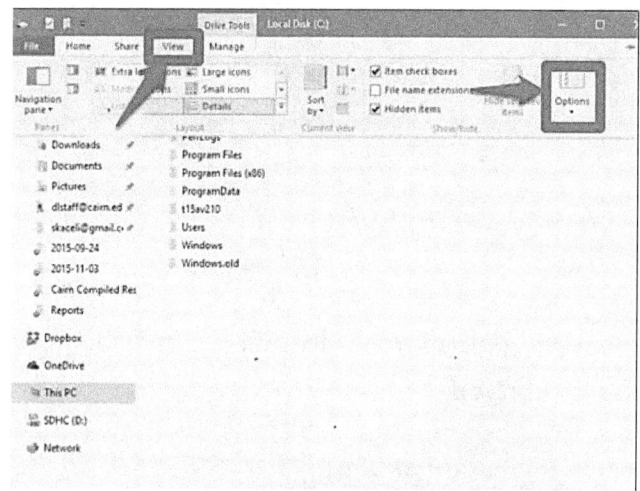

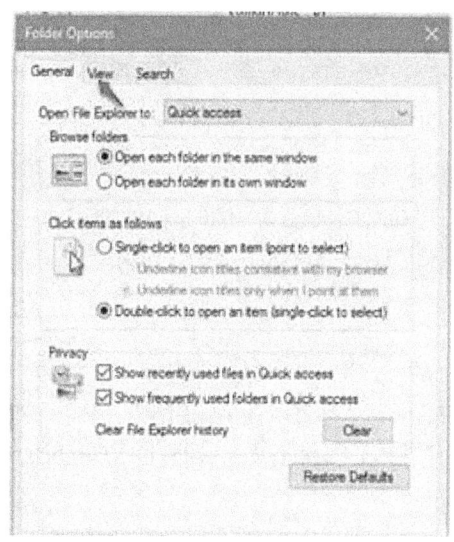

Click on "View" on the dialogue box that pops up – click on "Apply to folders" – It says "Do you want all folders of this type to match this folder's view settings? Click "Yes" and "Ok."

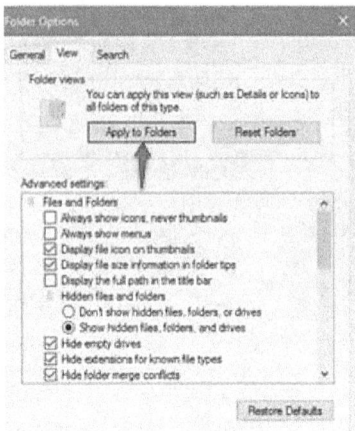

With this, the default view for all your folders on your computer is changed.

File Manager

We can use the task manager to identify problems in the computer and eventually resolve them or monitor the performance of the machine. Search for the "Task Manager" in the search box or right-click on the taskbar and click on "Taskv Manager" on the options that pop up. If you are opening the "Task Manager" for the first time, it displays minimal details – click on "More Details" to view other options as to what apps and background processes are running. If you wish to terminate a specific application from this list, click on it and select "End Task". This will kill that particular task.

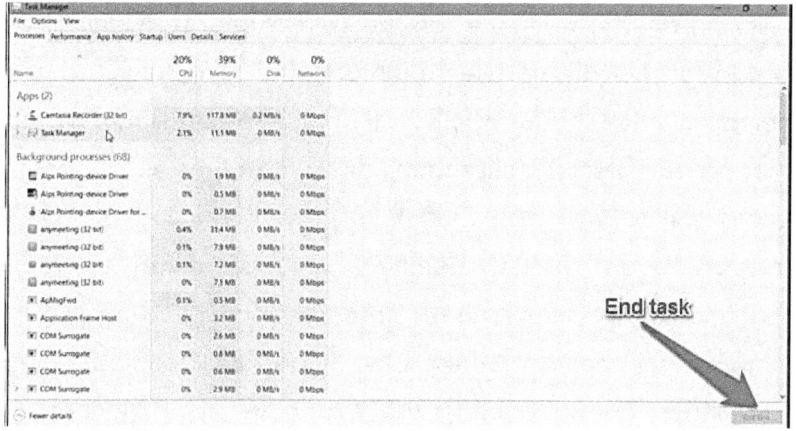

The Task Manager also shows application slowing down the PC by displaying the amount of CPU (process) they have taken. Typically, every app should be running between 3 - 4% on the CPU. If an app is running consistently at 15%, then these are app(s) slowing down or causing problems on your computer. You could also click on "Memory" to see which application is using up most of your computer memory. You can also identify if an app is taking more disk space than it should.

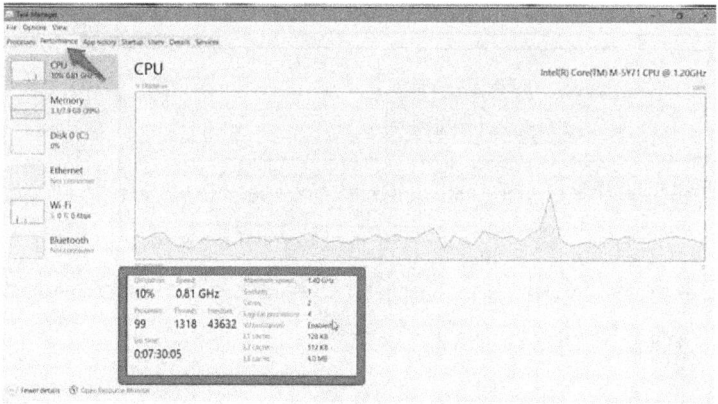

Clicking on "Performance" on the Task Manager Menu gives you a graphical representation of what is running on the computer, the CPU history, how many processes is running on the system, memory utilization, disk utilization, etc. In some cases you might notice that if your PC is running at 100% memory usage; you can identify what application is using up that memory or might need more memory, allowing you to troubleshoot memory issues. One important troubleshooting tool under "Performance" is the "Open Resource Monitor". It is located on the bottom-left side of the performance tab. When you click on "Open Resource Monitor", it provides more statistics on processes running, identifies issues in the PC and potentially resolving them. We will discuss troubleshooting memory issues in the troubleshooting PC section.

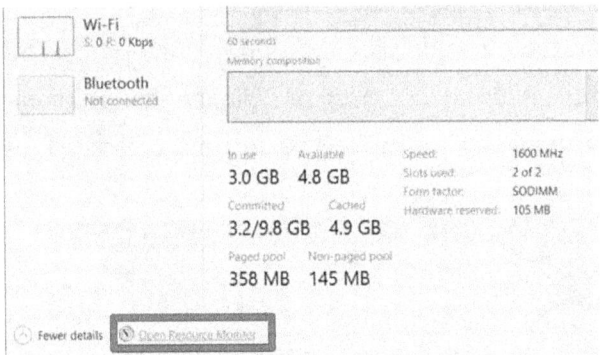

The other thing you can check on the File Manager is the "App history." This gives you a clue to how much CPU time and bandwidth different apps have utilized over a period or on a specific day or time.

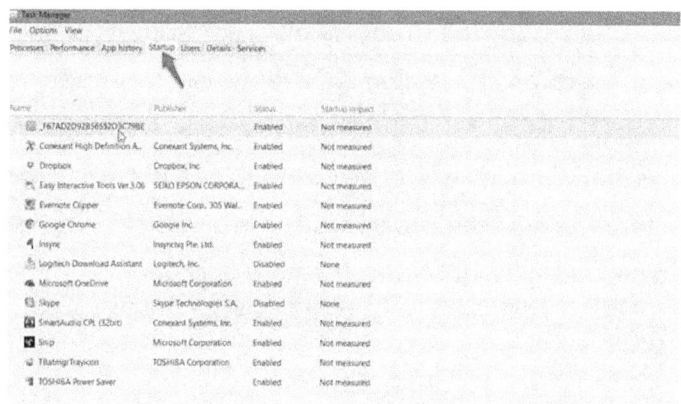

Under the "Startup" menu of the Task Manager, users can identify what program is starting automatically when the computer boots up and may choose to enable or disable them from this menu. To disable an app that starts up automatically, right-click on the app under the "Status" column and click on "Disable".

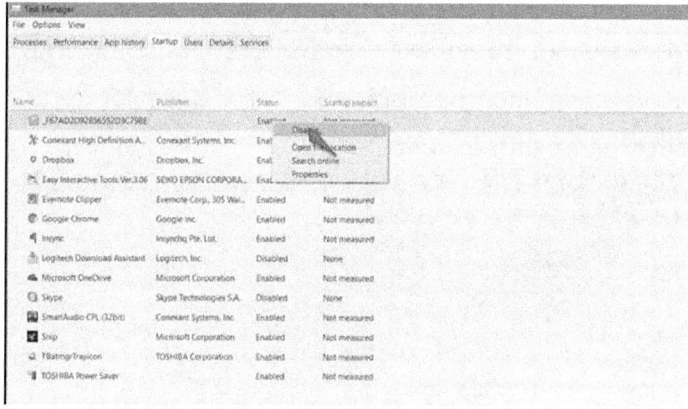

The next time you start up your computer, that app won't startup automatically except it is a virus or a spyware.

Under "Users" on the Task Manager, you can see the different users on the system and how much resources they are using. Clicking on "Details" in the Task Manager Menu displays details of every specific app that is running on the computer. It lists all the processes in the computer, their status, username, CPU utilization and Memory utilization.

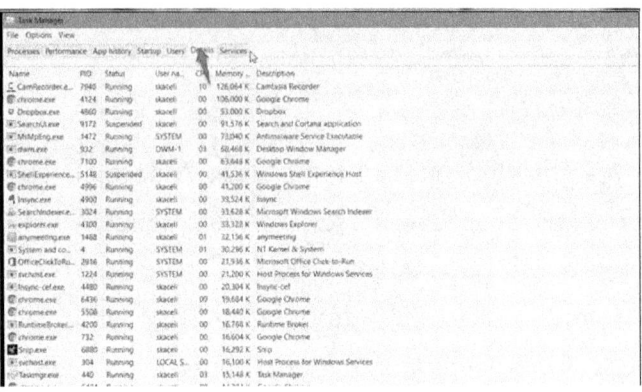

Under "Services" - you will have access to services running at the background. Be careful with this area, because stoppage of any service that needs to be running could disrupt the smooth running of the computer.

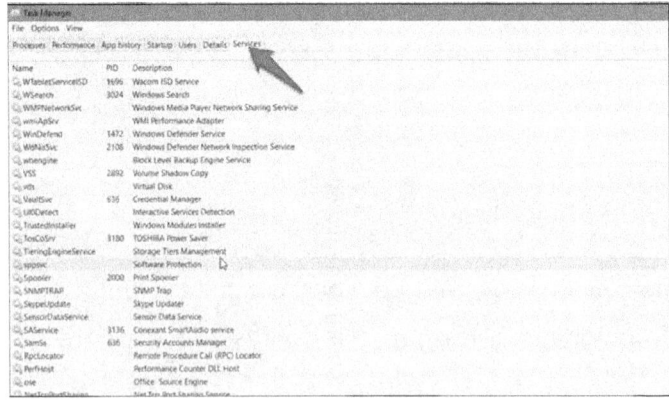

Before you stop any service, ensure to check on Google to know if there is any potential harmful effect of such action on the computer.

Customizing Privacy Settings

To customize Privacy Settings - press the windows key on the keyboard - in the searchbox type "Privacy."

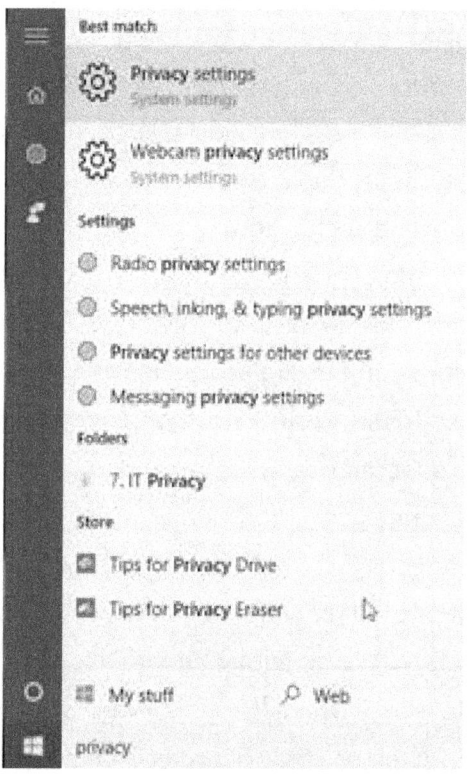

Some settings need to be disabled when setting up your PC for the first time. Ensure you turn them OFF to safe guard your personal information. Examples of "Personalization" information that needs to be disabled or turned OFF when setting up or upgrading the Windows 10 Operating System for the first time include -

1. "Personalize your speech, typing and inking input by sending contacts and calendar details, along with other associated input data to Microsoft."
2. "Send typing and inking data to Microsoft to improve the recognition and suggestion platform."
3. "Let apps use your advertising ID for experiences across apps."
4. "Let Skype (if installed) help you connect with friends in your address book and verify your mobile number, SMS and data charges."
5. For <u>Location privacy setting</u>, ensure you turn OFF "Find my Device and let Windows and apps request your location, including location history" and 'send Microsoft and trusted partners some location data to improve location services."
6. For <u>connectivity and error reporting</u>, turn OFF "Automatically connect to suggested open hotspots", "Automatically connect to networks shared by your contacts", "Automatically connect to hotspots temporarily to see if paid Wi-Fi services are available and "Send full error and "diagnostic information to Microsoft."
7. For "<u>Browser, protection and Update</u>, turn ON "Use SmartScreen online services to help protect against malicious content and downloads in sites loaded by

Windows browser and Store apps. However, turn OFF or disable the following – "Use page prediction to improve reading, speed up browsing, and make your overall experience better in Windows browsers. Your browsing data will be sent to Microsoft" and "Get updates from and send updates to other PCs on the internet to speed up app and Windows update downloads."

With the above settings taken care of during installation or upgrade of the Windows 10 Operating System, you can further manage your privacy settings in the "Privacy Settings Menu". As earlier stated, you can access this menu by typing privacy in the search bar and click on "Privacy Settings".

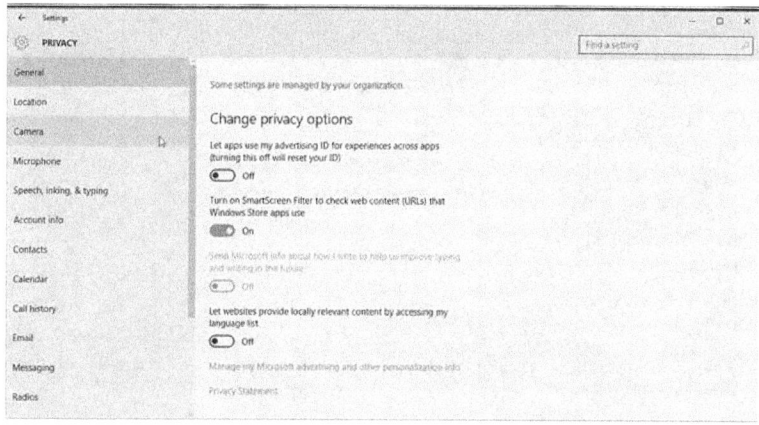

For <u>location</u>, turn OFF Location to prevent Microsoft or other PCs with GPS capabilities from tracking your location. You should also clear the "location history" if you have toggled ON location in the past.

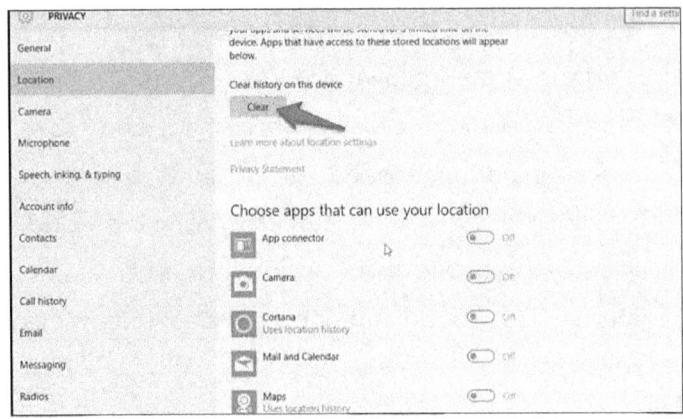

You can also choose to turn OFF the location App from multiple Apps running in the system. Also, don't allow Apps to use your camera except they have your permission.

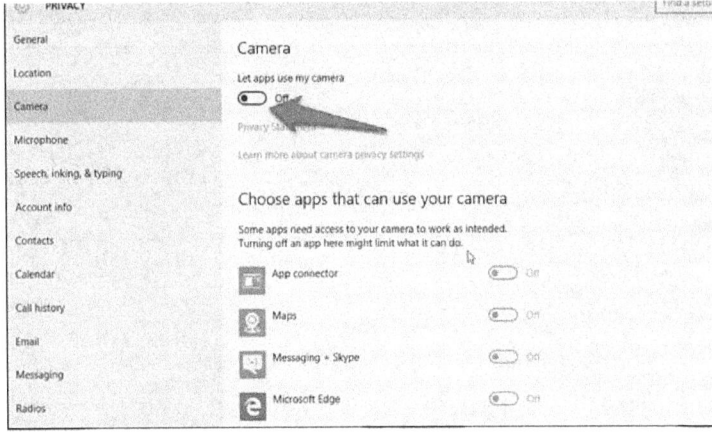

You can choose to enable the camera and turn off apps that shouldn't use it without your approval.

For "Speech, inking & typing" also known as "Get to know me." This is a setting that Microsoft uses to get to know users better. They want to know what your calendar is, what you are doing, what you are searching for, what you are typing etc.

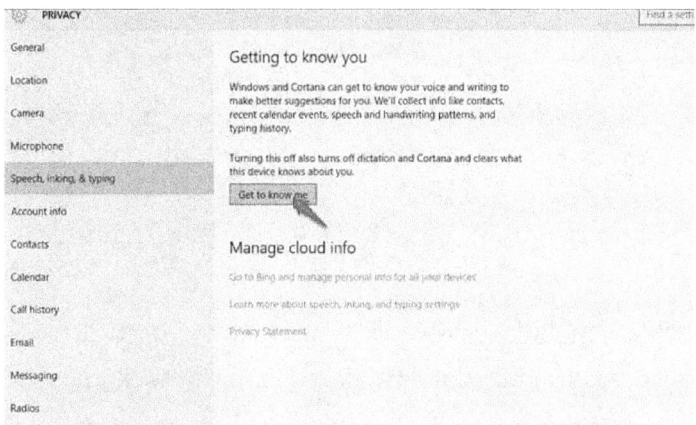

If you are concerned about your privacy, you can choose to turn it OFF.

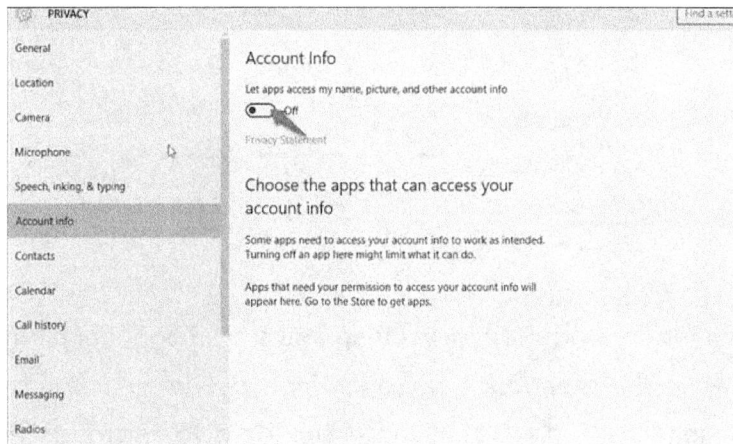

Turn account information OFF - this is to prevent apps from accessing your name, pictures and other account information. Under contacts, you can determine whether certain apps can utilize your contacts. Same goes for your calendar.

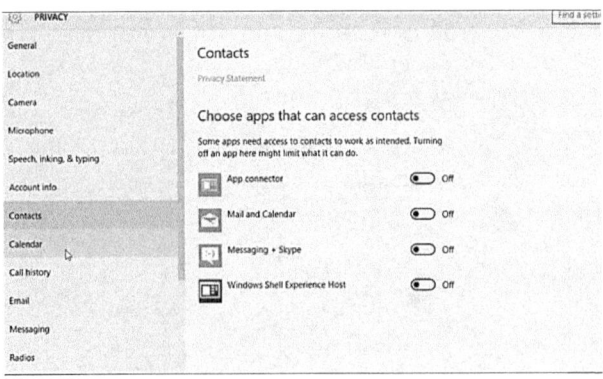

Enabling call history will allow messaging apps like Skype have access to your call history. By turning the Radios ON in privacy settings, you can determine what app could control your radio like Wi-Fi connectivity, hotspots, etc.

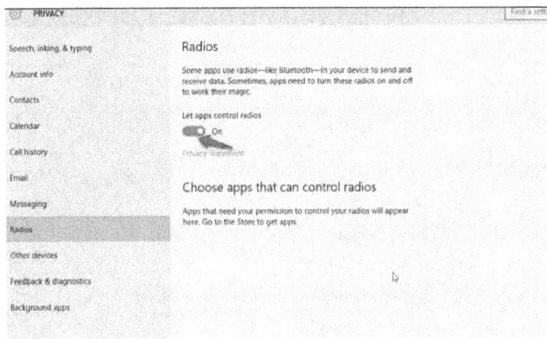

Another important privacy setting you should consider turning down is the "Feedback & diagnostics". By default, Windows will send "Full" diagnostic and usage data to Microsoft. My suggestion is to change it to "Basic". This will only send basic diagnostic and usage data to Microsoft. In the "Background apps" menu, you can enable/disable apps that should run at the background.

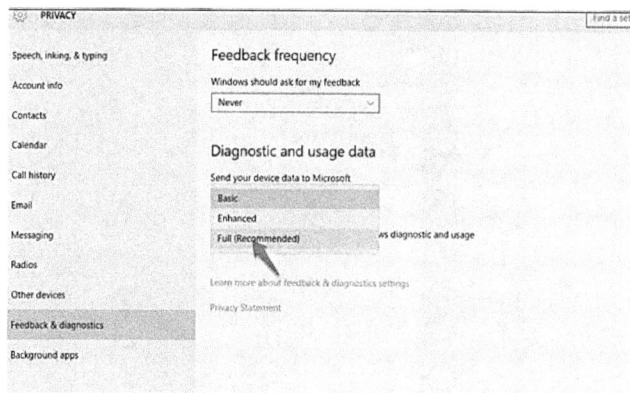

Another thing you can do in the privacy window is to search for all privacy settings that can be customized - In the Privacy window's search box at the top-right corner type in "privacy," this will provide a list of all the privacy settings options as shown below.

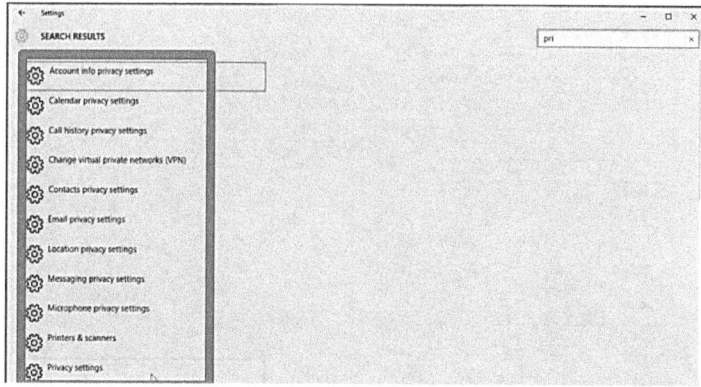

Network and Internet Settings

There are settings under the network and internet settings that you may choose to customize. To do this, in the search box on the taskbar, type "Change Wi-Fi Setting." Scroll down and click on "Advanced Settings."

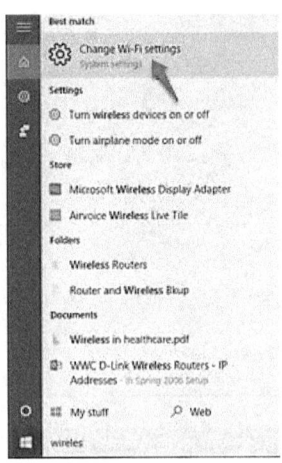

Here you can customize several wireless options. For example, if you want your PC to be discoverable, you should turn ON the "Allow your PC to be discoverable" option.

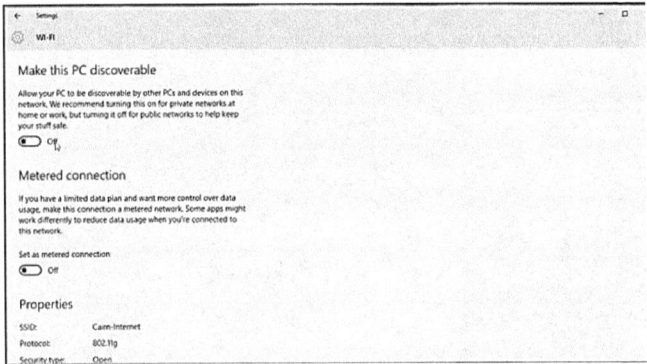

You can also manage the data utilization of devices or computers connected to your PC by turning ON metered connection. This will enable you to share data with each connected device. Another network setting option you can customize is Wi-Fi Sense. In the "Network & Internet" window, click on "Manage Wi-Fi Settings" and make the necessary changes.

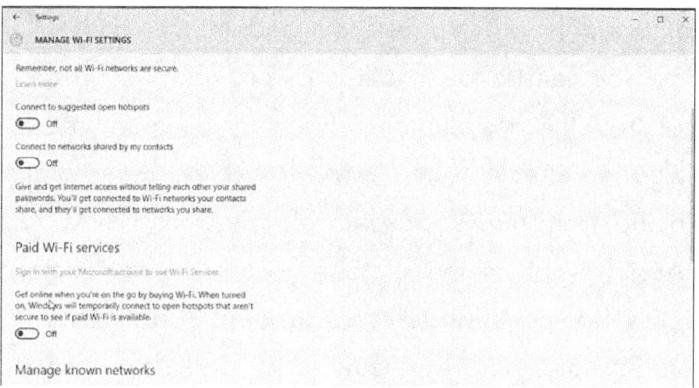

How to Lock Your Computer

If you share a space in your office or at home and you don't want unauthorized access into your PC when you are not around, you can lock your computer. To do this, hold down the Windows key and the "L" key on the keyboard. At this point, if you click on the screen, you will need to input your password to access the desktop or where you left off.

How to Install Windows 10 on MacBook Pro

Windows 10 Operating System can be installed on a MacOS with the aid of software called Bootcamp. Before you get started, ensure your Mac is compatible with the newest version of the Bootcamp installation process. You can check this by clicking the Apple logo in the upper-left corner of the screen and click on "about this Mac". As long as you have a 2015 Mac (or later) or a 2013 mac pro (or later), you are good to go with the installation process. If you have a Mac older than those years, you will still be able to install Windows Bootcamp, but your process may look a little bit different from the steps outlined in this book. To get started, you need a legitimate copy of Windows 10 and ISO format for this installation. This can be purchased and downloaded directly from Microsoft website. If you choose to download from the Microsoft web page, ensure you select the April version as the October version is not compatible with this Bootcamp installation process - also select your language - select "64-bit download" and download should start automatically.

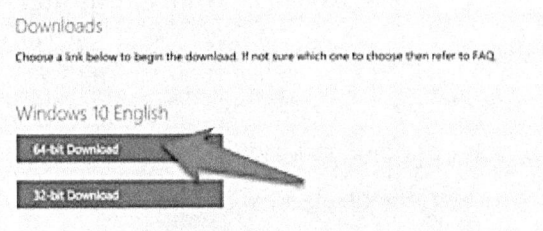

Start by opening up the Bootcamp assistant by searching for it in "Spotlight." Once the Bootcamp assistant is open, follow along with the prompt that is displayed. If you have an older mac, you will need to be guided with the process of creating a Windows 10 installer on a separate USB drive. Follow the prompts and Bootcamp will handle the rest for you. If you are using a newer mac, you will be prompted to locate the Window 10 ISO file on your system or Bootcamp will automatically detect it. Below that, you will be prompted to allocate a portion of your drive storage space for the Windows Operating System and the files.

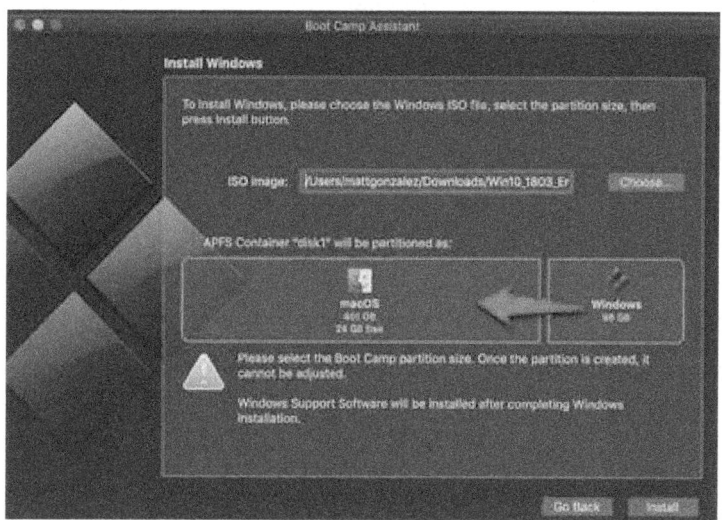

Simply drag the size of the box to adjust the partition of each Operating System's storage space. If you want more space for your Mac's applications and documents, keep the Mac box larger and vice versa if you want windows larger. Next, Bootcamp will download some additional drivers and software. This will also divide the space on your internal drive. While this process is going on, Bootcamp will prompt you for your admin password to finish things up. Mac will restart automatically and you will be taken to the setup portion of Windows 10 - select your language and click "Next" - If you purchased a product key, type it into the product key box - choose the version of Windows you wish to install - Carefully read and agree to the licensing agreement - you may be prompted to install disk for Bootcamp partition. From the lists displayed on the screen, choose Bootcamp and select the eraser icon next to the format button and click "OK" - click

"Next." The Window will then go into the installation process. This will take a while to complete. - After a short while, Mac will reboot and come up with the setup portion of Windows 10 - follow the process to input your region, user account, password etc. When this is complete, you will be taken to the Windows 10 desktop, a box will open up automatically prompting you to download some additional Bootcamp drivers to get Windows working correctly with all of Mac peripherals and internals. Follow the prompts and allow everything to install. When this is done, go to the Windows 10 start menu and type "Update" in the search box and click on the "Check for update" option. Windows 10 will download all available updates and install them. This will also take a while to complete depending on the size of updates that needs to be downloaded. Windows 10 will reboot and you are done. You now have a fully functional Windows partition on your Mac.

If you are in Windows and you wish to head to MacOS - go to the bottom-left corner of the display and click on the Bootcamp icon and select "Restart to MacOS". If you wish to switch between MacOS and Windows, restart your Mac and hold down on the "Option key" until you see the Apple logo. You now have two options to choose from.

New Features and Capabilities of Windows 10 version 1903

It is no longer news that Microsoft recently carried out a major update on the Windows 10 Operating System on the 10th of May 2019. If you are still running the older version, go to the Windows Update & Security page under "Settings" - click on "Check for updates" and it will install Windows 10 update. In this section, we will be looking at changes made to the User interface, Apps & Experiences, Input & Accessibility and other new options in the Windows Settings in the new update.

Windows & Theme

After setting up a PC running the May 2018 update, for the first time, you will be greeted by a new default Wallpaper. The themes in the new Windows 10 update looks brighter and flatter. The search box no longer holds a microphone icon because Cortana is no longer bound to Windows search. Cortana is now separated from the Window search experience and she has her icon in the taskbar. The purpose of separating Cortana from the Search bar is to develop a more focused search User Interface. Cortana, on the other hand, seems to be a victim of neglect with these changes. Her User Interface hasn't changed much. However, Cortana can now be hidden or displayed on the taskbar independent of the search box and a lot of the conversational ability with Cortana is no longer accessible by typing into the search box. Although with this separation of Cortana from the search box, you won't lose any of the search functionality previously provided by Cortana because the web preview pin powered by Bing is capable of spitting out quick answer to most of your simple questions.

Some of Cortana more useful commands like setting up reminders or toggling settings can still be accessed from the search box if you are very specific about the command syntax. The separation between search and Cortana goes beyond the taskbar. In Window Settings, "Search" now has its dedicated section on the landing page.

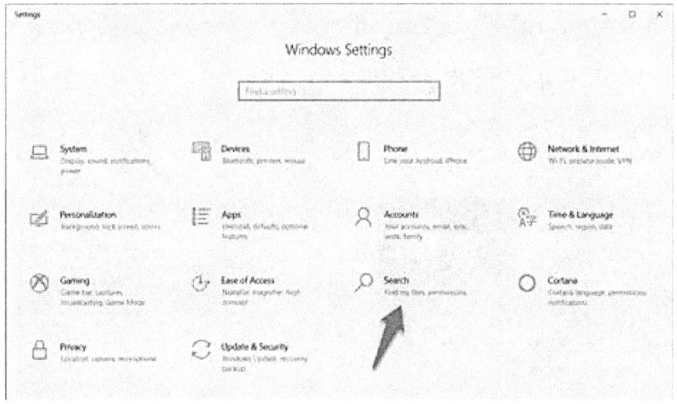

In the search settings, you can customize the settings of your search results, clear search history or configure the Windows search indexer. The May 2019 update provides a new enhanced option for the search indexer.

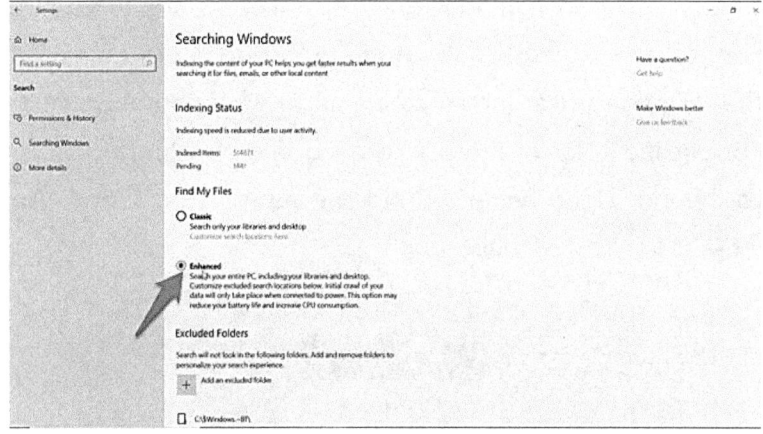

With "Enhanced" enabled in the search indexer settings, all the files in your PC will be indexed. This is in contrast to previous releases of index where only files in the main libraries are indexed.

Also with the new update, there are now three base color theme options in the Windows personalization settings - Dark, light and Custom.

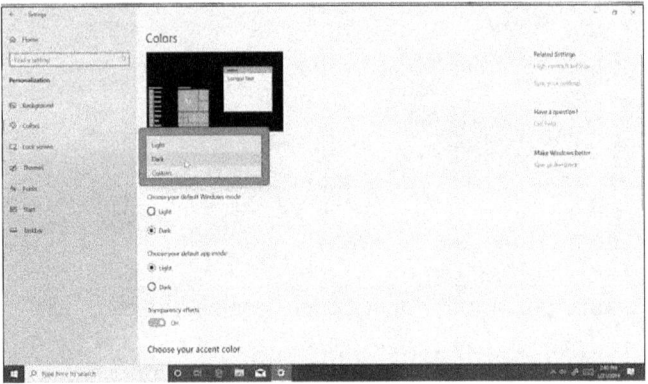

Custom is selected by default and expands to two daughter settings - "Windows mode" and "App mode". Windows mode changes the appearance of the taskbar, start menu and other Windows User Interface elements while the "App mode" changes the color of the background in supporting Apps. Just like the old "Light theme", "Windows mode" is dark and "App mode" is light by default.

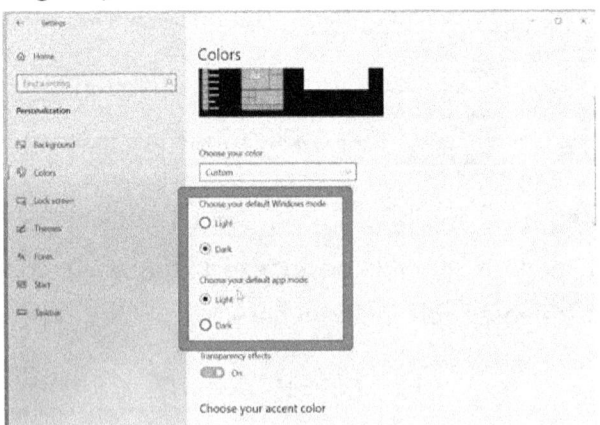

However, with the new options in the May 2019 update, you can switch to an entirely new light beam for everything including the taskbar, start menu and action center.

Context Menu such as those opened from the start menu and action center now features a fluid design with background, connecting animations, drop shadows, highlights and reveal effects. You will notice more fluid design throughout the system's User Interface in apps like settings and lock screen. These visuals are part of Microsoft's fluid designs system which continues to spread throughout Windows despite been unveiled almost two years ago.

Action Center & Screen Brightness

Requested by Windows users since Microsoft unveiled it in 2014, Action Center now has a brightness slider in the new update.

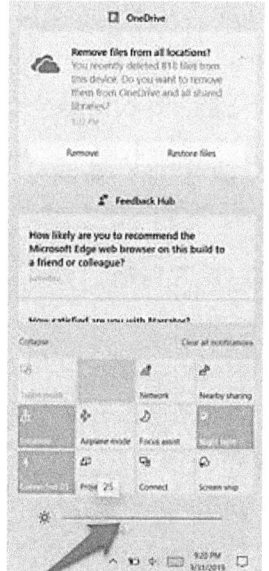

The brightness slider has granular control over screen brightness, allowing you to increase/decrease brightness. Screen brightness profiles have also been removed in the May 2019 update. Before the update, Windows Operating System had two distinct brightness profiles – when it is plugged to a charger and when the charger is removed and the PC is on battery. Notice that when you plug your laptop to a charger, the screen brightness increases and decreases when on battery. With the May 2019 update, the brightness setting in the action center is the only brightness profile, and it won't change when you connect or disconnect your charger.

Start Menu

Fresh installation of the May 2019 Windows 10 update comes with a new default start menu layout. These changes will not affect you if you are only updating your PC. The new design is more organized. If you want to get rid of all the default apps and replace them with yours, you can unpin entire groups by right-clicking on their headers and selecting "unpin group from Start."

Other UI Changes in New Windows Update

Some other notable UI changes are
1. The new icon on the taskbar when the PC doesn't have an internet connection.
2. Files and downloads have been categorized and sorted by date.
3. The clipboard User Interface using "Windows key + V" is more compact.

4. There is now a DPI awareness mode in the "details" tab in task manager, which you can enable to explore which apps are/are not DPI-aware.

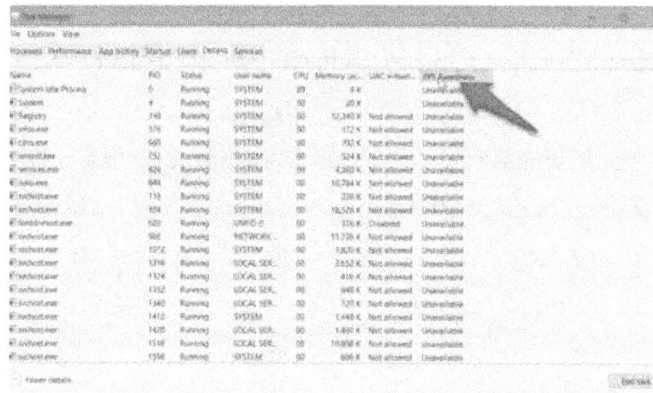

5. There is also an option in Task Manager to set default tab

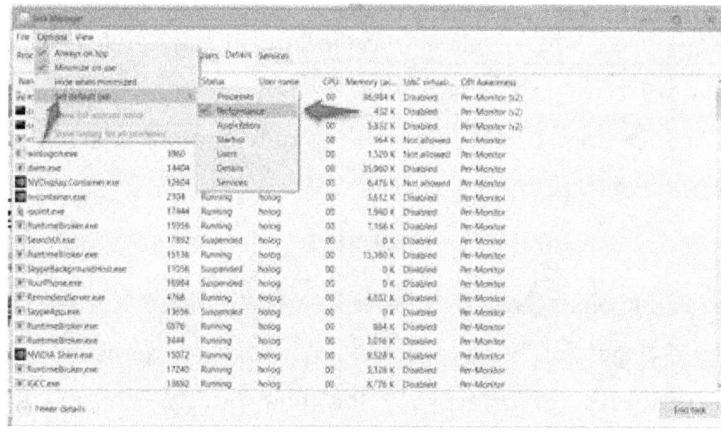

6. The start menu now runs its process called "StartMenuExperienceHost.exe," which improves the reliability of launching the start menu.

Apps & Experiences

Many Apps and experiences can now be removed with the May 2019 update. Apps like 3D viewer, calculator, calendar, Groove music, Mail, Microsoft solitaire collection, Movies & TV, My Office, OneNote, Paint 3D, Skype, sketch, sticky note, voice recorder and weather can be uninstalled directly from the Start Menu. However, if you change your mind in the future, these apps can always be downloaded from the Microsoft Store.

Snip & Sketch

Many people complained that snip and sketch in the October 2018 Windows 10 update were too soon and some useful options were removed. In the May 2019 update, these options are back. Window snip mode and more delay options are now available when taking a new snip. Additionally, options for snip outline, an entirely new feature are found in the app settings.

Notepad

The classic old notepad is here to stay, although, in the new update, it got a few new tricks you might find useful. Notepad now displays an asterisk in the title bar of an open file whenever there are unsaved changes. There are also some new keyboard shortcuts for opening notepad window with Ctrl + Shift + N, Ctrl + shift + S to save a notepad file and Ctrl + W to close the notepad window. When saving a notepad document, you now have "UTF-8" and "UTF-8 with BOM" in the encoding options. Where BOM stands for Byte or a marker.

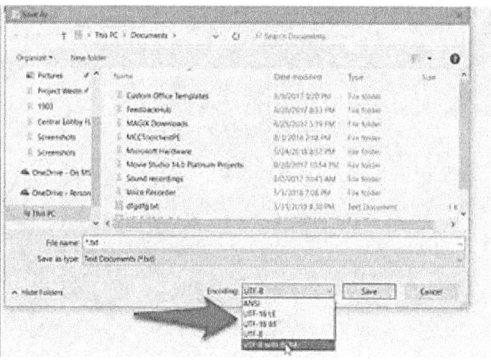

Stick Notes

In the new Windows 10 update, Sticky notes now match the color theme of your PC. In Dark mode, the body of sticky notes appears dark with a colored stripe along the top. A new color - Charcoal gives light theme users the option to have dark notes along with the more traditional ones.

Game Bar

The Game Bar accessible with "Windows key + G" now has a shortcut in the capture section beneath the capture options. From the option, you can view, rename or delete captures with your games. "Open File Location" button at the lower right corner of the game bar takes you directly to where the captured files are saved.

Windows Mixed Reality

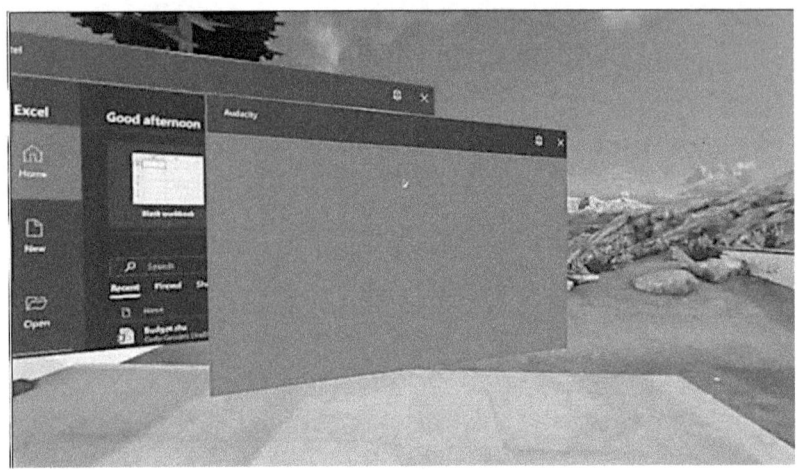

For some time now, universal windows app has been available to run in the windows mix reality environment. Now, you can open and interact with legacy desktop apps in Windows Mix Reality just like their UWP counterparts. Running legacy apps in this environment is still experimental, so some apps might not work as expected.

Windows Sandbox

Windows Sandbox is a new virtual desktop environment for Windows 10 pro and enterprise in the update. Setting up a Sandbox is simple, unlike creating a virtual machine; Sandbox doesn't require an external installation of windows. It can be enabled in the Pro and Enterprise from the Windows Feature Dialogue. You can read more about how windows Sandbox work on the Windows internals page on Microsoft web page.

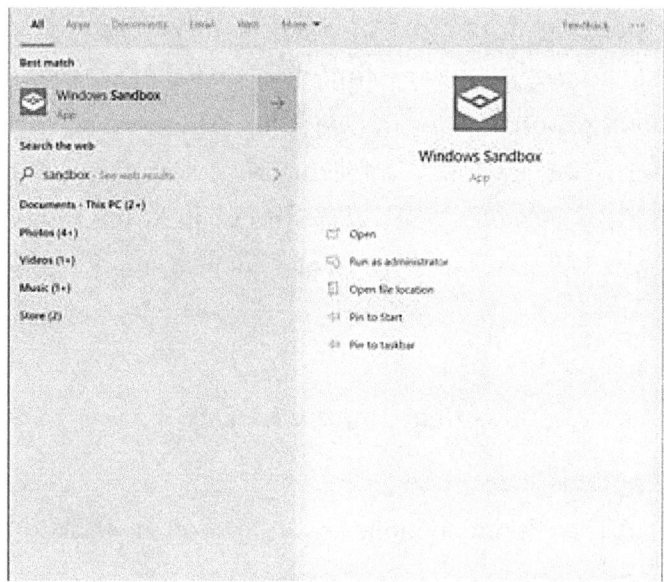

Other notable changes to Apps & Experiences include:
1. An updated User Interface for the universal printing dialogue.
2. The mail and calendar apps now have a full dark mode expanding to more areas in each app.
3. A new Office App to replace the old "My Office App."
4. Raw Image Extension which improves raw file support in the file explorer is now available in the Windows store.

Input & Accessibility

Interacting with your device at tablet mode is not as difficult with the improvements made on the touch keyboard in the May 2019 update. The keyboard has its animations back, fluidly popping in and out of sight when you tap into a text field. Enhanced swiftkey integration also improves the touch keyboard experience in this update. When typing with the keyboard, the Swiftkey intelligence adjusts the write-ups dynamically to improve accuracy. This swiftkey intelligence for the touch keyboard is now available in various dialects of English, French, German, Italian, Spanish, Portuguese and Russian.

Other Input Changes

Other notable input changes include:
1. A New Hindi phonetic keyboard option which is available in more languages.
2. A new Japanese input method editor
3. ADLaM and Osage Keyboard support

Narrator

A new narrator home launches every time you turn ON narrator. Narrator home allows you to access all the narrator settings. From the settings menu, additional voices and other languages can be downloaded without having to download entire language packs. This can be done in the narrator settings by navigating to "Add more voices" - click on the voice language and click "Add." A new setting called "Hear advanced information about controls when navigating" like "Hear advanced details like help text on buttons and other controls" lets you adjust what information you can hear about the controls. ^08\1\2019_ * OSTERisk

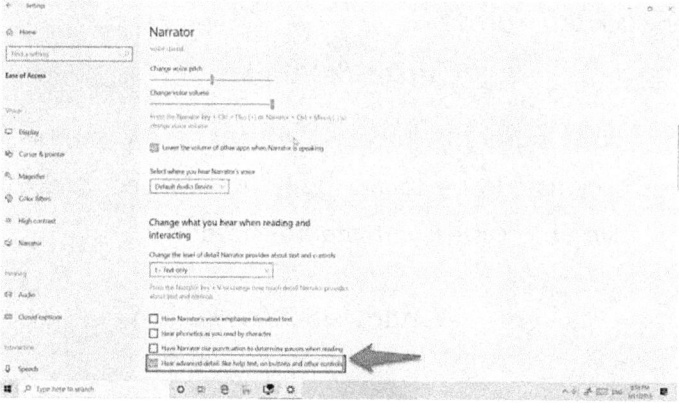

It is disabled by default in this update. However, when enabled, users can adjust how robust it should be from 0 - 5 using the keyboard shortcut "Narrator Key + V." ^09\1\2019_

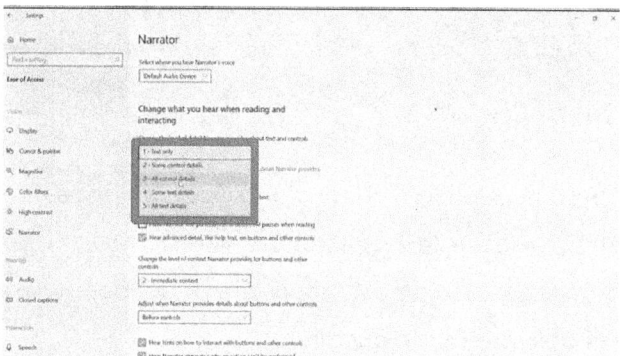

In a previous release of Windows 10, a feature that allows you hear characters read phonetically in the narrator was added, however, Microsoft took note of the feedback provided by users and decided to turn this feature OFF by default. Now, you can activate phonetic reading on demand with the keyboard shortcut "Narrator Key + double comma (i.e. hitting the comma key twice)." Additional narrator options can be found in the Windows settings under "Ease or Access" - then click on "Narrator."

Cursor & Pointer

Also in the "Ease of Access" Settings, New cursors and pointer options can be found. Both the size and color of the pointer can be adjusted with the new update.

Windows Settings

In the System section under "Focus assist," there is a new automatic row to mute notifications while using an app in the full-screen mode. Automatic rows are situations where focus assist will activate automatically.

In the storage section of Windows Settings, a new layout for the storage page breaks down storage usage by type.

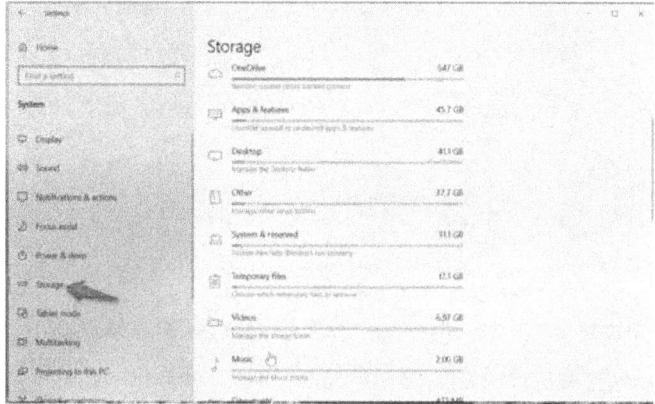

In the Accounts section of Windows settings, a new setting page for Sign-in option is added. In the personalization section of Windows settings under "Fonts" – you can now drag and drop new fonts on this page to install them in the new update.

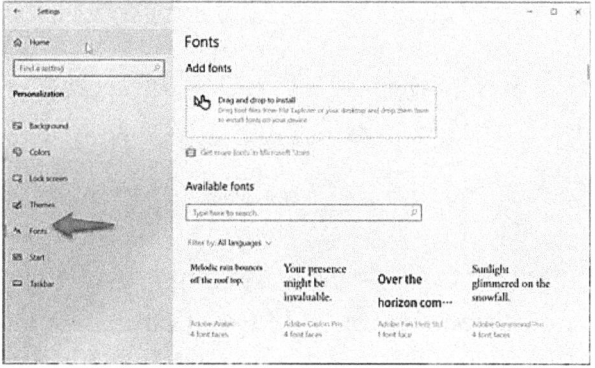

In the Network & Internet section in the windows settings, under "Ethernet," advanced settings and information are now available for Ethernet connections.

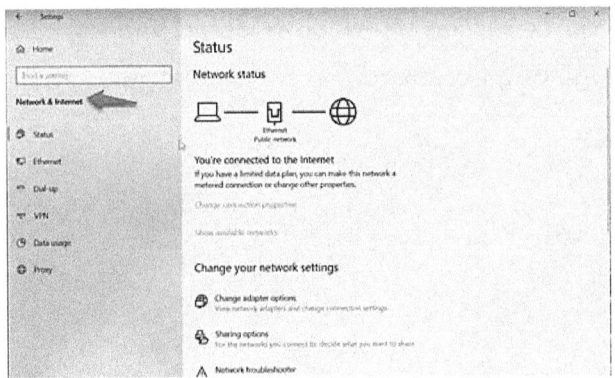

The Update and security section in the Windows settings has a redesigned settings page for "Windows update". Active hours can be adjusted dynamically based on your usage, with a toggle.

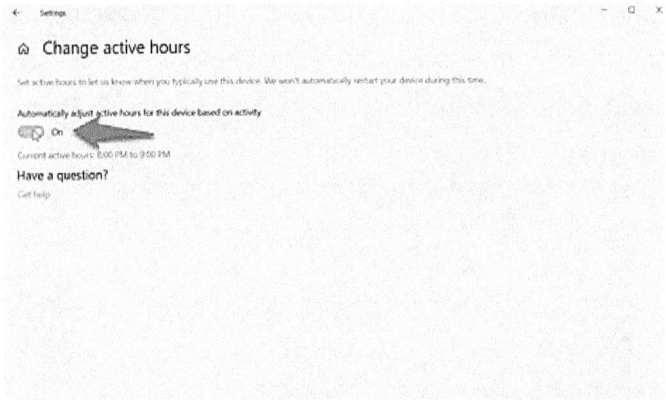

During these hours, Windows won't update automatically. You can also pause updates for up to seven days using the "Pause updates for 7 days" button.

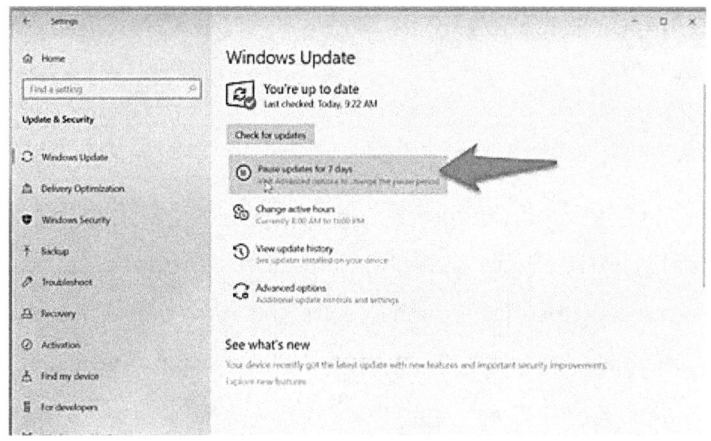

Finally, there is a new page for the Window's insider program.

Other Tips and Tricks

Dark Themes

If you want to give your PC a more stylish look including a dark theme, you have several options - Click on "Start" - "Settings" - "Personalization" - in the left panes, select colors - For the theme, the default is "light" - Select "Dark."

Game Mode

If you are a PC gamer running a lower spec system, the game mode will help improve your experience. It allows more of your system resources to be allocated to your game, which prevents background processors from disrupting your experience. This also works with non-windows store games too. Click on "Start Menu" - "Settings" - "Gaming" - In the left panes click on "Game Mode" - Turn ON "Use Game Mode".

Storage Sense

Over time your PC could be filled up with needless clutters without you knowing it. But in the latest update, Microsoft added storage sense which clears out unneeded temporary files and files that are more than 30 days old in your recycle bin. Go to "Settings" - Select "System" - Select "Storage" in the left pane - Turn On Storage Sense - Click on "Change how we free up space" and have all the options turned ON.

Night Light

Night light is a program that removes blue light. To activate night light, in "Settings", select "System" - under color, turn ON "Night light." If you are running a multiple monitor setup, this option will turn ON/OFF night light on all monitors. If you select "Night light settings," there are several options to customize your experience. You can adjust the color temperature, set night light to only operate during sunset to sunrise hours, or you can set your hours.

Shop with Edge

Microsoft edge rowser has a new feature that helps users get a better deal when shopping online on stores such as BestBuy, Amazon, etc. Visit the online store - select an item you wish to purchase - when you land on the product page, a notification will appear at the top right corner of the edge browser - Click on the notification and it shows you the prices of the same product on other retailers platform, to enable you identify a retailer with a cheaper offer for the product.

Print to PDF

With Microsoft's Print to pdf app, you can now save any document to PDF without using third party software.

Virtual Desktops

This feature has been available on the MacOS for a while but just introduced to Windows. Virtual Desktops allows you to have various versions of your PC's desktops. To create a new virtual desktop, Click on "Task View" on the taskbar - Click on the Plus sign "+" to add a new desktop. To go back to your previous desktop, click on "Task View" again and select "Desktop 1". You can also move opened programs to other desktops - Click on "task view" - Click and drag the open program from "desktop 1" to "desktop 2." You can also drag the program to the plus sign to create a new desktop environment.

Emoji

On Windows 10, you can use emojis by using the on-screen keyboard - Right-click on the taskbar - and enable "show touch keyboard button - select the keyboard - click on the emoji icon and choose from the variety of emojis.

God Mode

If you want the ultimate settings control panel, then you will find God mode useful. Originally introduced in Windows Vista, God mode is easy to set up. Create a "New folder" by right-clicking on the desktop - select "New" - "folder" - Rename the folder using "GodMode{ED7BA470-8E54-465E-825C-99712043E01C}" - hit the enter key. Double click on the new icon on your screen and you will find several settings you can play with.

Useful Hot Key Combinations for Windows 10

Key Combination	Action
Windows Key ⊞ + CTRL + D	Open Virtual Desktop
Windows Key ⊞ + CTRL + Left/Right Arrow Keys	Switch between Virtual Desktops
Windows Key ⊞ + CTRL + F4	Close a Virtual Desktop
Windows Key ⊞ + M	Minimize all Open Apps
Windows Key ⊞ + Comma	Take a peep at Desktop
Windows Key ⊞ + "a number Key from 1 - 9	Open an App from the TASKBAR
Windows Key ⊞ + Left Arrow and Windows Key ⊞ + Right Arrow in each app window	Split Screen between two Apps
CTRL + ALT + TAB or Windows Key ⊞ + TAB or ALT + TAB	Switch between Apps
CTRL + SHIFT + ESC	Open Task Manager
Windows Key ⊞ + E	Open File Explorer
Windows Key ⊞ + Plus or Minus Key	Open Magnifier App

Key Combination	Action
Windows Key ⊞ + Print Screen	Take Screenshots
Windows Key ⊞ + A	Open Action Center
Windows Key ⊞ + I	Open Settings
Windows Key ⊞ + C	Open Cortana in Listening Mode
Windows Key ⊞ + G	Windows Game Bar
Windows Key ⊞ + ALT + R	Start/Stop Recording in Game Bar
Windows Key ⊞ + ALT + B	Start Streaming Recorded scene in Game Bar
Windows Key ⊞ + L	Lock Down PC
Windows Key ⊞ + SHIFT + M	Restore Minimized Apps
Windows Key ⊞ + O	Lock Device Orientation on tablets
Windows Key ⊞ + P	Switch Operating Mode for External Display
Windows Key ⊞ + Q	Open Search Bar
Windows Key ⊞ + R	Open Run Dialogue Box
Windows Key ⊞ + T	Switch Focus to Taskbar
Windows Key ⊞ + U	Open Utility Manager
Windows Key ⊞ + W	Open Windows Ink Workspace
CTRL + F6	Cycle Application Windows

Key Combination	Action
CTRL + W	Close File Shortcut
Right-Click Mouse on taskbar + D & U	Cascad or Uncascad Files
Right-Click Mouse on taskbar + E	Stack all Opened Windows
Right-Click Mouse on task + U	Undo Stack all Opened Windows
Alt + F4	Close Application
CTRL + N	Open New Application Window
CTRL + SHIFT + N	Create New Folder
Right-Click Mouse + W and Select	Create New Office Files
Alt + Left Arrow or Left Arrow	File Explorer Navigation
Alt + P	Preview File in File Explorer
Alt + Double-Click	File or Folder Properties
Windows Key ⊞ + SHIFT + S	Screen Clipping

Shutting Down your Computer

Click on the "Start menu" - "Power" - "Shut Down." You could also follow the same process to put your PC to sleep or restart the entire system. Alternatively, you could shut down your computer by right-clicking on the "start menu" - "Shut down or sign out."

Troubleshooting Problems

In this section, we will look at common software problems on the Windows 10 Operating System and how to troubleshoot them. Hardware Troubleshooting is not covered here. It takes a competent technician to fix hardware issues to avoid permanent damage on the PC.

Keyboard Not Working

Keyboard not working is a common problem faced with Windows 10 Operating System. There are several ways to fix this problem, but the easiest is - Click on "Start" - "Settings" - "Ease of Access" - "Keyboard" - Turn ON "Filter Keys" this automatically turns On other options under it. - Under the Filter Keys, Turn OFF "Beep When keys are pressed or accepted" and "Display the Filter Keys icon on the taskbar" - Restart your PC and the keyboard not working issue is resolved. If this method does not fix the problem, carryout addition troubleshooting by Right-Clicking on the Start Menu - Click on "Device Manager" - Click on the Keyboard to extend it - Right-click on the keyboard icon and select "Update Driver Software" - click "browse my computer for driver software" - Select "Let me pick from a list of device drivers on my computer" - Select "Standard PS/2 Keyboard" and Click on "Next." This will install the latest update for your Keyboard.

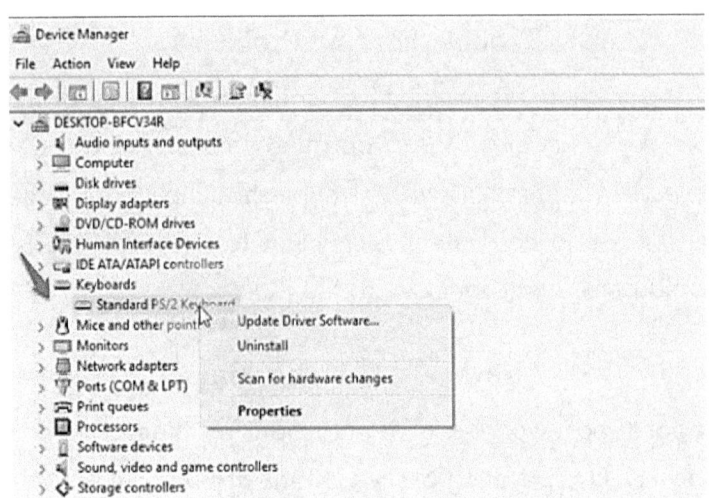

Troubleshoot blue Screen

A Blue screen occurs when the CPU is starved of sufficient power. To fix this, while the computer boots press the F2 function Key on the Keyboard - navigate to "Advanced Voltage Settings" - "CPU Core Voltage Control - With the Plus sign "+" on the keyboard, increase the Voltage of the CPU Vcore above the default voltage (1.100volts should be Okay).

Troubleshoot Memory Leak

Whenever you run a program, it requires processing power or Memory to run its operations. After a program is done and you close the application, what it is supposed to do is release those memory allocations to the system for other programs to use. However, when there is a Memory leak, a limited amount of memory is made available or there won't be any memory at all for other programs to utilize. This is referred to as Memory leak. To fix this click on "Start Menu" - in the search box, type in "regedit" - Right-Click on the "regedit - Left Click on "Run as administrator." If the User Account Control Window pops up, select "Yes."

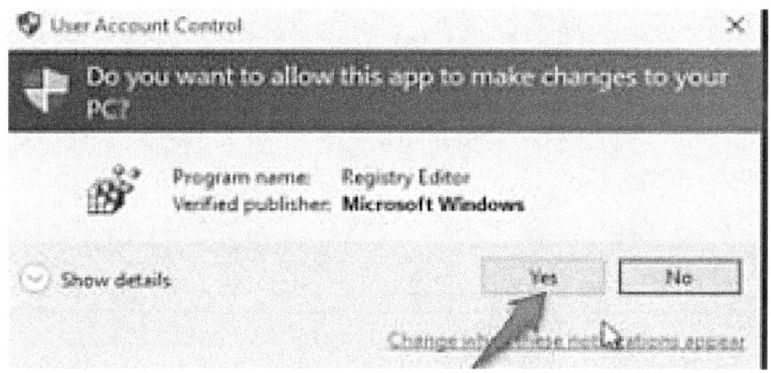

In the Registry Editor window, Click on the drop-down arrow next to the HKEY_LOCAL_MACHINE.

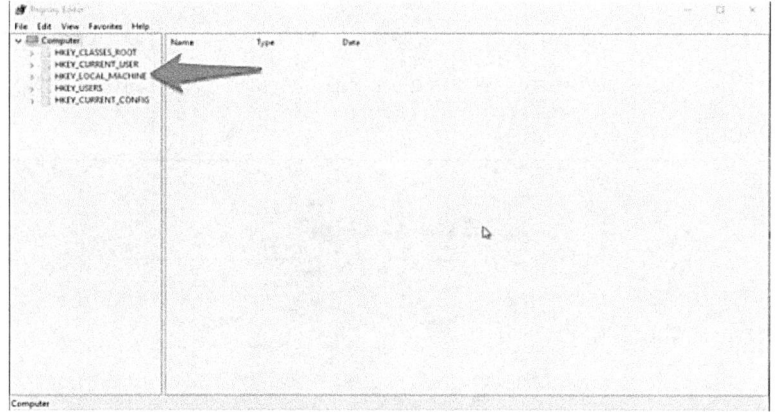

Left-Click on the little drop-down arrow Next to "System," then click on the little drop-down arrow next to "ControlSet001"

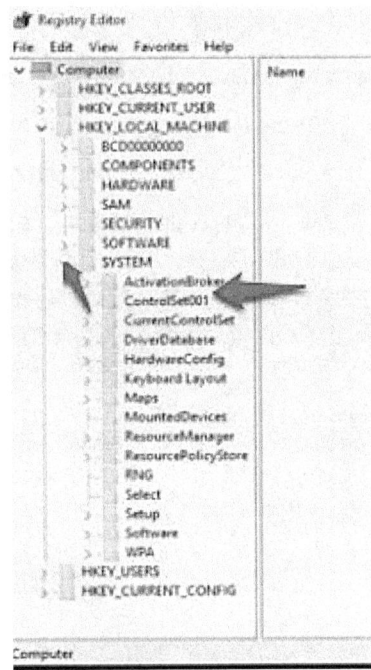

Next, click on the Little drop-down arrow next to "Services" - Scroll down the list until you get to Ndu." - On the right side of the "Ndu" window, right-click on "Start" and Left-Click on "Modify"

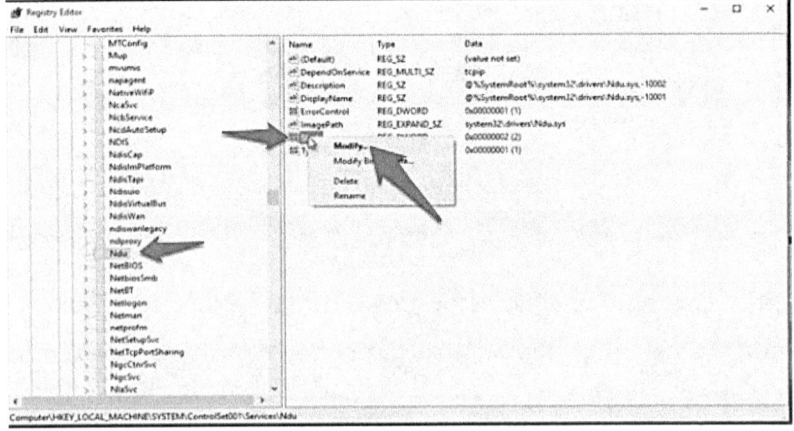

This will open the "Edit DWORD value window

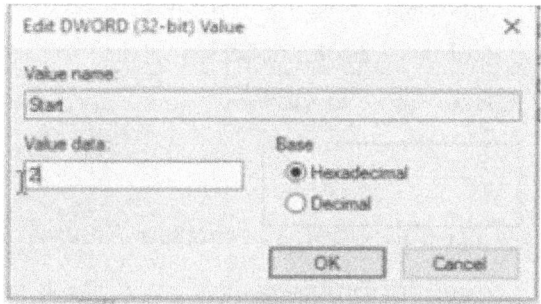

Increase the Value data from the default number to four (4) and click on OK. Another method to prevent memory leak is as follows - Right-Click on the "Start Menu" - Select "Run" - type "Services.msc" in the "Open Box" - With the service window open, Scroll down to "Superfetch" and left-click on it.

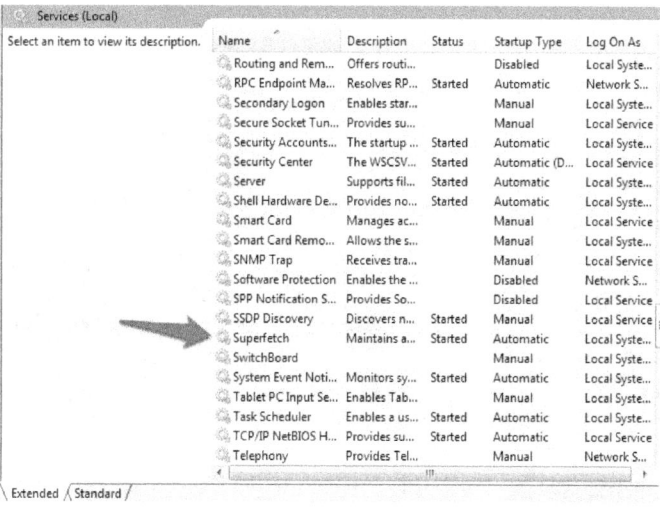

On the right, the description says "Maintains and improves system performance over time. - Now Right-click on Superfetch and Left-click on "Stop" - Left-Click on "Superfetch again" - In the "Startup Type", click on the drop-down arrow and select "Disabled" - Click "Apply" and "OK." This will prevent Superfetch to be launched anytime you start up the computer. Close the service window and restart your computer.

Troubleshooting Start up issues

There are a variety of problems that could result in Windows 10 having start-up issues. When Windows 10 has a start-up problem, it becomes difficult for the Operating System to boot to the Desktop and you may keep powering your PC ON and OFF. After three consecutive Power OFFs are done improperly, Windows 10 will launch the "Automatic Repair" tool.

"Automatic Repair" is built into Windows as a recovery option tool for your computer. You get a message "Your PC did not start correctly," and you are expected to click on "Restart" to fix the problem, which in most cases does not resolve the issue. The "Advanced option" is a better option to try out especially when Windows Operating System refuses to boot to the desktop. Click on the "Advanced Option" - Click on "Troubleshoot."

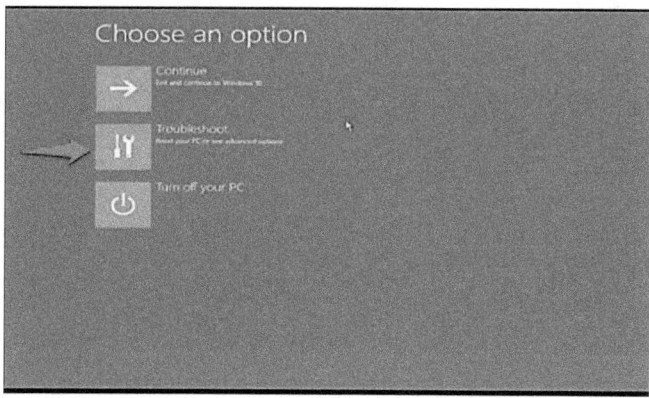

Nest, Select "Advanced Options"

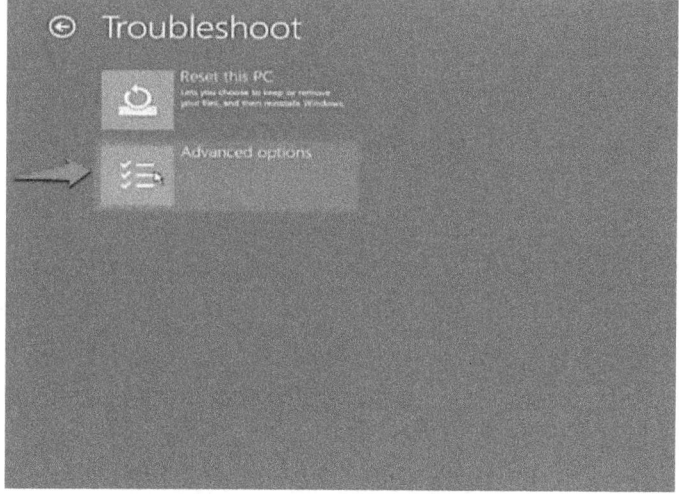

Click on "System Restore." This will take you to a dialogue window saying "System Restore can help fix problem that might be making your computer run slowly or stop responding. System restore does not affect any of your documents, pictures or other personal data. Recently installed programs and drivers might be uninstalled."

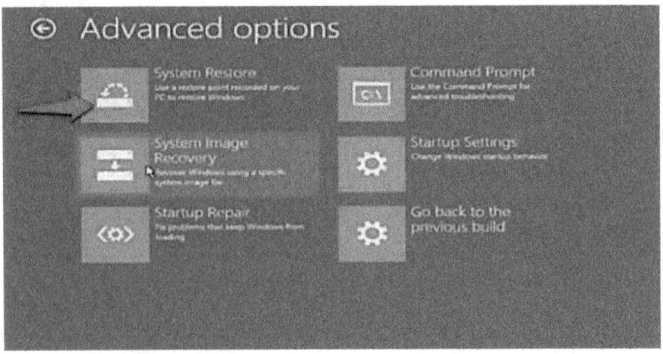

This is an important point to note, if you know any program that you installed recently that is causing this issue, it is highly recommended to boot into safe mode and uninstall the program or driver. But if you don't know what caused it, select "Next."

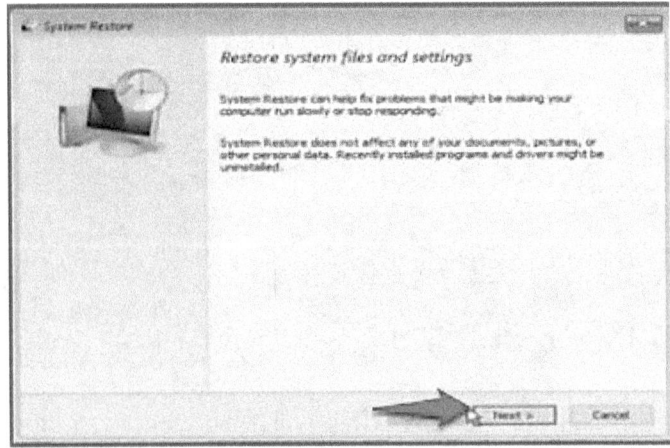

Windows will display one or more system restore points with a time stamp you can select from and click "Next."

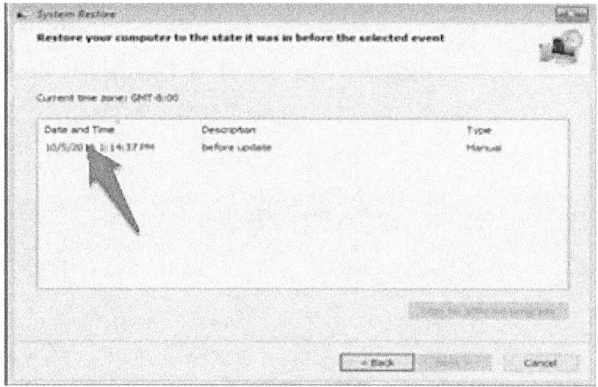

Click "Finish." You will receive a warning saying, "Once started, System Restore cannot be interrupted, do you want to continue?" Select "Yes," and it will begin to initialize the System Restore. This will take a couple of minutes. Click on "Restate." If this method does not work, there is another option to consider - go back to the automatic repair window - click on "Troubleshoot" - "Advanced options - this time around, instead of selecting "System Restore," click on "Startup Repair" -

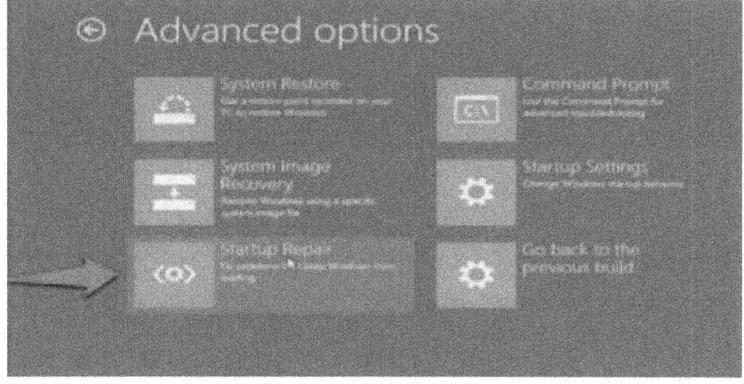

This will take a little time to diagnose your computer and fix the problem. If this option doesn't fix the problem, here is a third and final option. Click on "Advanced options" on the "Automatic Repair window"- Select "Troubleshoot" underneath "Choose an option" - "Advanced Options" - "Command Prompt."

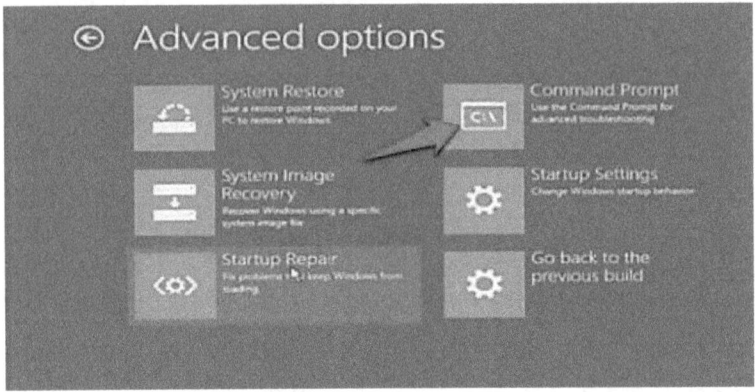

This brings up the Command Prompt Window.

In the Command Prompt window, type "C:" without the quotation mark and hit "enter" on the keyboard. This will open the C drive. While in the C drive, type in "dir" without the quotation mark "C:/>dir" and hit the "Enter" key on the

Keyboard. This will display the PefLogs, program files, users, Window and Windows.old. In some cases, it might be the D drive. Next, type in "cd\windows\system32\config" without the quotation mark and hit "Enter" on the keyboard. It should look like this;

C:\> cd \windows\system32\config

Next type "md backup" without the quotation mark and hit "Enter" on the keyboard.

C: \windows\system\system32\config>md backup

Next, type "copy *.* backup" and hit enter. Note: there is a space between "copy" and the first asterisks as well as between the last asterisks and "backup."

C: \windows\System32\config>copy *.* backup

Next, type "cd regback" without the quotation mark and hit "Enter on the Keyboard.
Now you are under the regback, type in "dir" again and hit "Enter" on the Keyboard.
At this point type "Copy *.* .." (i.e. Copy (space) asterisks dot asterisk (space) dot dot.) and hit "Enter" on the Keyboard again.

For "override" you will need to override all so type "A" on the keyboard without the quotation mark. Hit "Enter" key. At this point you are good to go, close the command prompt window

Click on "Continue" on the "Automatic Repair" Window.

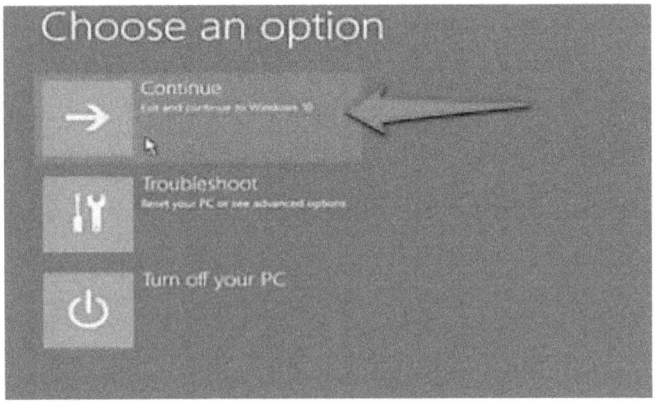

One of the above steps should help resolve your Windows start up issue.

Wi-Fi Not Connecting

If your PC is not connecting to Wi-Fi, you can troubleshoot it using the steps outlined - Click on "Start Menu" and in the search box type "Control Panel" and left-click on it - In the

"Control Panel", click on the category next to "View by" at the top-right side - Select "Small icons"

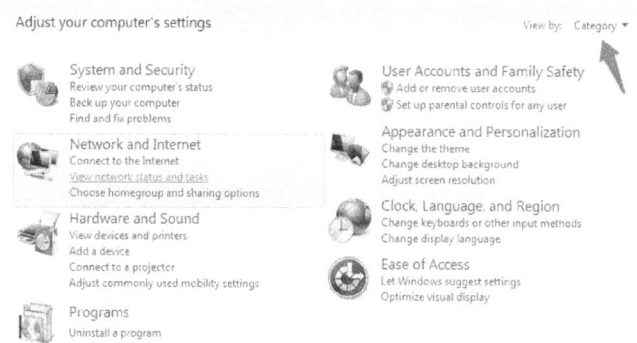

Click on "Internet options" on the list of settings option

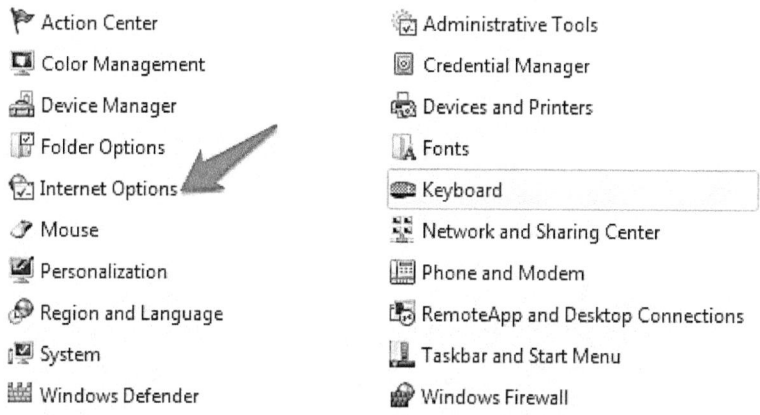

In the Internet "Properties dialogue" box, click on "Advanced"

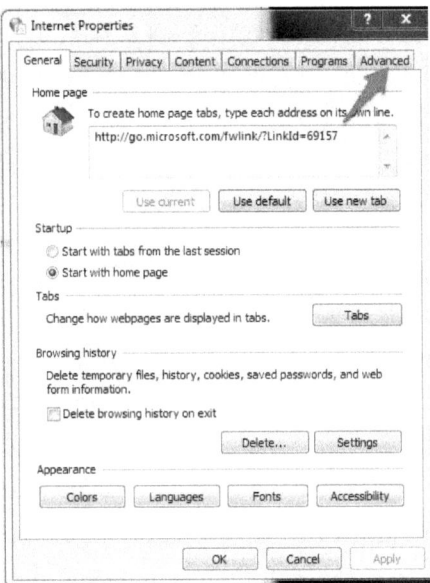

Click on "Reset"

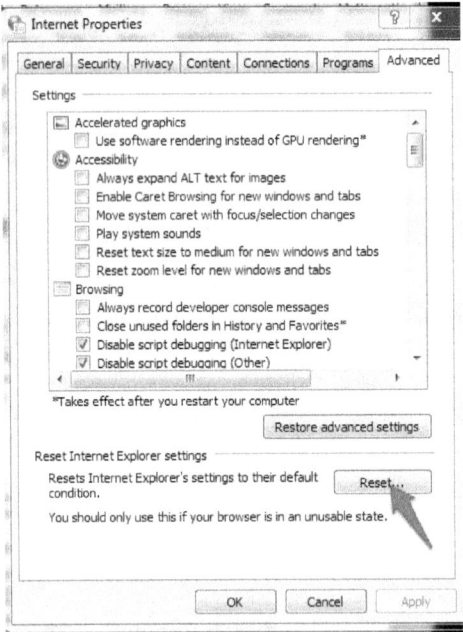

Check the "Delete Personal Setting" box and click on "Reset"

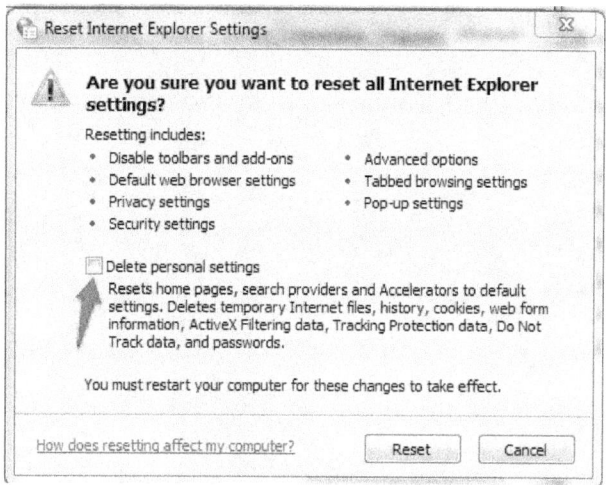

Close the "reset Internet Explorer settings" dialogue box. Next - Right-click on the "Network Icon" on the taskbar and click on "Open Network and Sharing Center" - Click "Change adapter settings" at the right side - Click on the "Wireless Network Connection or Wi-Fi" On the options bar, click on "Enable the network device."

Troubleshooting Wi-Fi disconnecting frequently

Click on the "Start Menu" - in the search box, type in "Device Manager" and left-click on it - Click on the little drop-down arrow by "Network adapters" - Right click on the wireless adaptor "Intel® 82574L Gigabit Network Connection" and left-click on "Properties" - On the dialogue box that comes up, click on "Power Management" - Uncheck the box that says "Allow the computer to turn off the device to save power" and left-click on "Ok". - Close the "Device Manager" and restart your computer. Check if this resolves the problem. If this does not resolve the problem, take the next option - Click on the "Start Menu" and in the search box type in "Power Options."

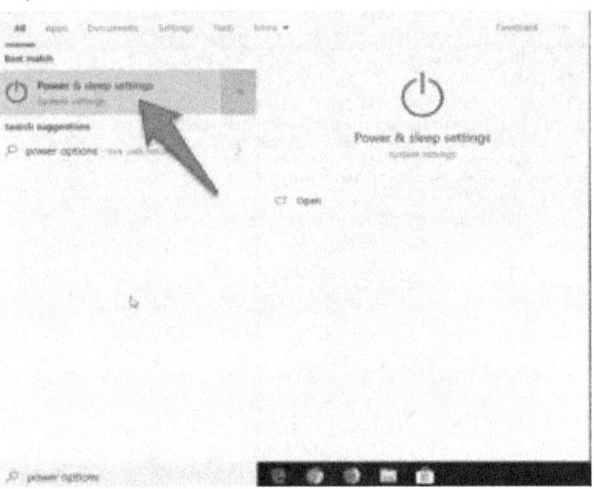

Left-click on "Power & sleep Settings"

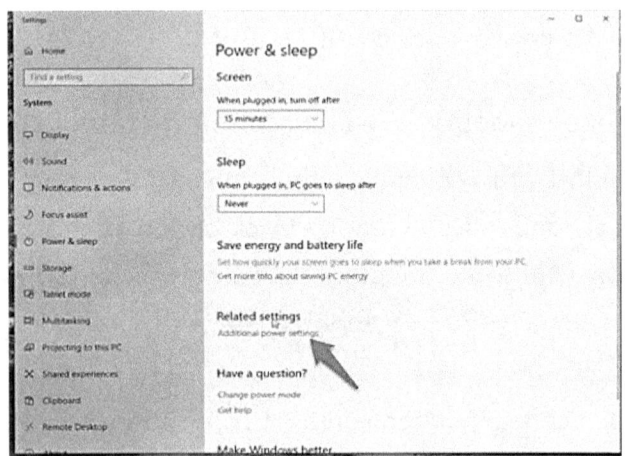

In the "Power & Sleep" setting dialogue box, under "Related Settings" Click on "Addition power settings" - Check "High Performance" and click on "Change plan settings" next to "High Performance" - Left-Click on "Change advanced power settings" - In the "Power Options" that pops up, click on the plus sign "+" next to the " Wireless Adaptor Settings" - click on the plus sign "+" next to "Power Saving mode" and keep the "Settings" to "Maximum Performance" - Left-click on "OK" - close the Windows and restart your computer.

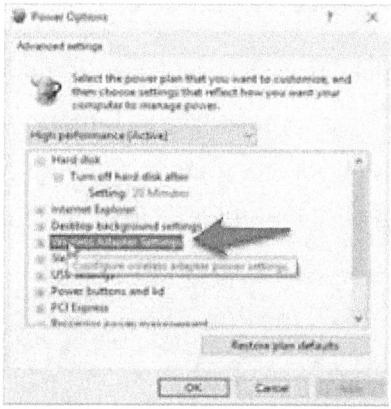

Remote Desktop Connection not Working

First in this troubleshooting process is to enable remote desktop - Click on "Start menu" - "Settings" - "Remote Desktop" - Turn ON "Enable Remote Desktop" and "confirm" - Scroll down to "User accounts" and click on "Select users that can remotely access this PC" - Click on "Add" - you can type in a particular desktop address you wish to add or type "Everyone" in the "Enter the object names to select" then click "Ok."

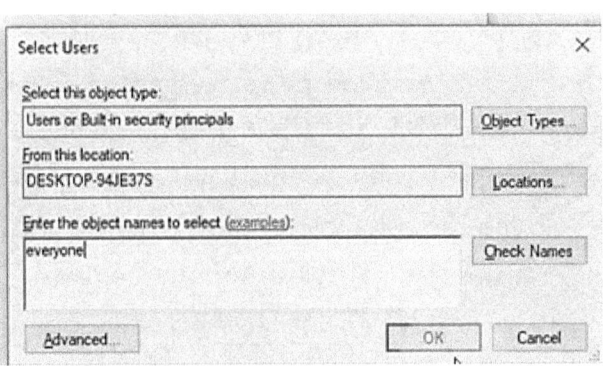

Click "ok" again. If this method does not work, the next option is - Right-click on "This PC" - scroll down and click on "Properties" - Click "Remote Settings" - Check "Allow remote connections to this computer" - then uncheck "Allow connections only from computers running Remote desktop with Network Level Authentication (recommended)."

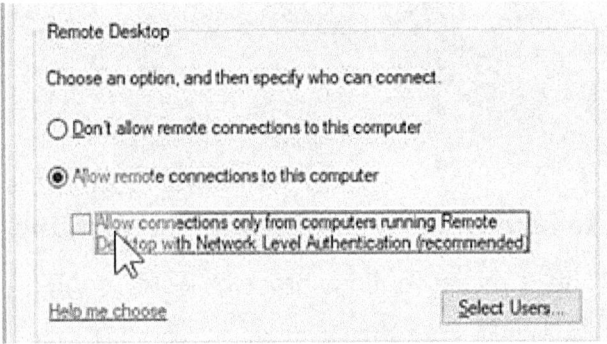

Click "Apply" and "Ok." The third method is as follows - Click on "Start menu" - in the search box type in "Firewall" and click on "Windows Defender Firewall" - Click on "Advanced Settings."

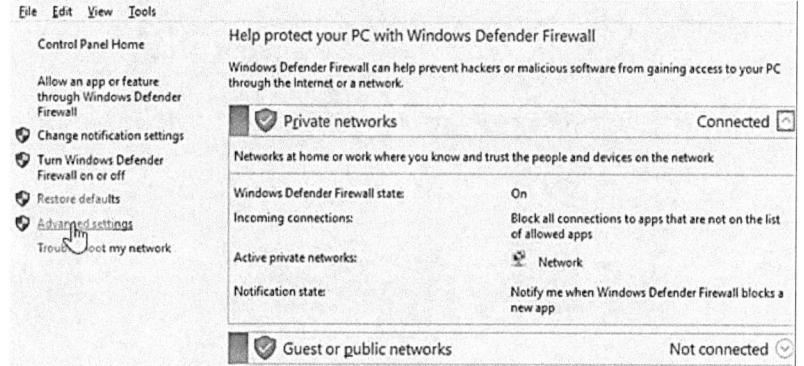

Click on "Inbound Rules"

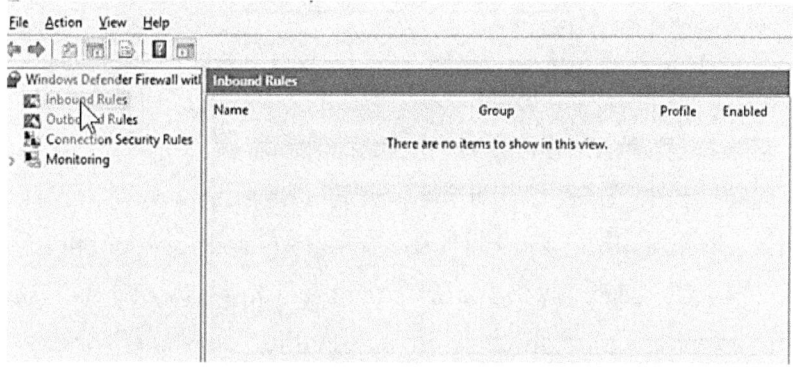

Scroll down and search for "Remote Desktop - Shadow (TCP-in)", right-click on it and click on "Enable Rule" - Again, right-click on "Remote Desktop - Shadow (TCP-In) and click on "Properties" - click on "Advanced" and in the Edge traversal section, click on the drop-down arrow and select "Allow edge traversal."

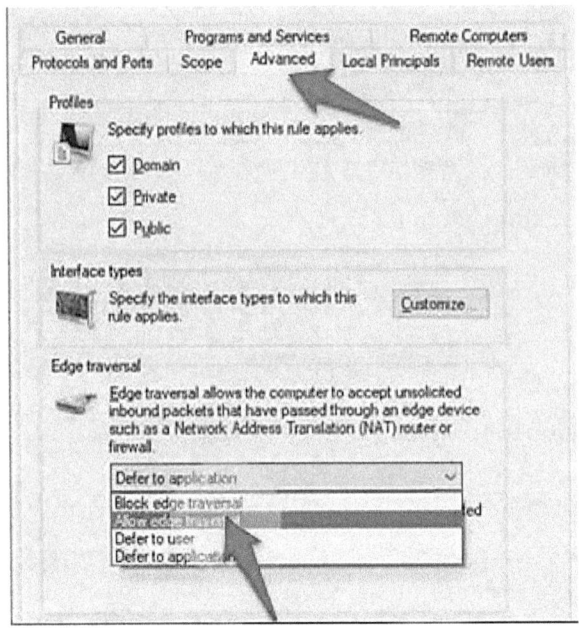

Click "Apply" and "Ok." If the problem persists, we will look at the fourth method to troubleshoot remote desktop connection problem. - Click on the Start Menu - in the search box type in "Services" and lift-click on it - In the "Services Window" Scroll down and search for "Remote Desktop Services" and double -click on it - Change the "Startup type" to "Automatic" - Click on "Stop" and "Yes". If you are still having issues - Right-click on "Network."

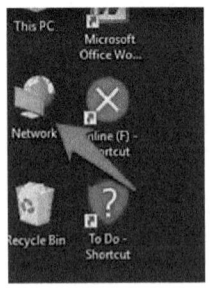

And click on "Properties" - "Change adapter settings" - Right-click on "Ethernet" and select "Properties" - Uncheck "Internet Protocol Version 6 TCP/iPV6) - Click "Ok."

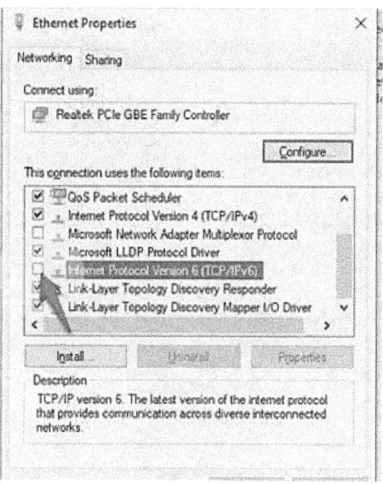

Mail App Not Working

Click on "Start Menu" - in the search box type in "Apps & features" and left-click on it - Scroll down to "Mail and Calendar" and left-click on it.

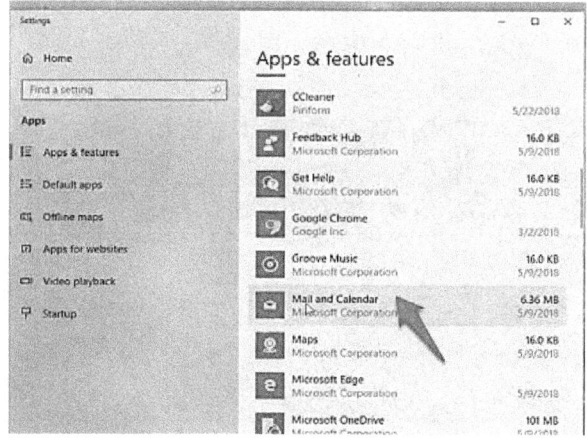

Left-click on "Advanced Options" underneath the Mail and Calendar" - scroll down and click on "Reset underneath "Reset." This troubleshooting method will not delete your mail but resolve any issues with the Mail and Calendar app.

Complete Clean, format or reinstall Windows 10

Before resetting your PC, backup your important files, documents and pictures. Left-click on the Start button - in the search box type in "Reset" and left-click on "Reset this PC" - On the settings window, click on the "Get Started" button.

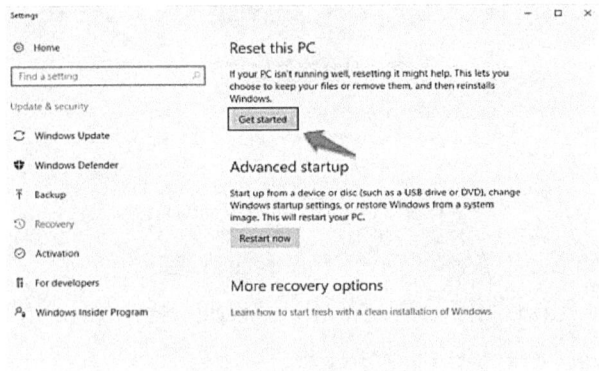

You have two options there after - "Keep my files" and "Remove everything" - Select "Remove everything"

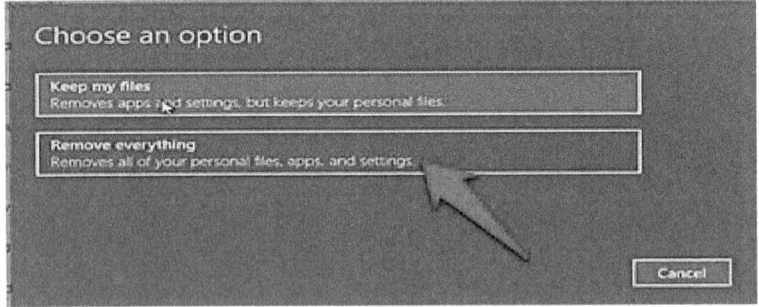

Next, click on "Just remove my files"

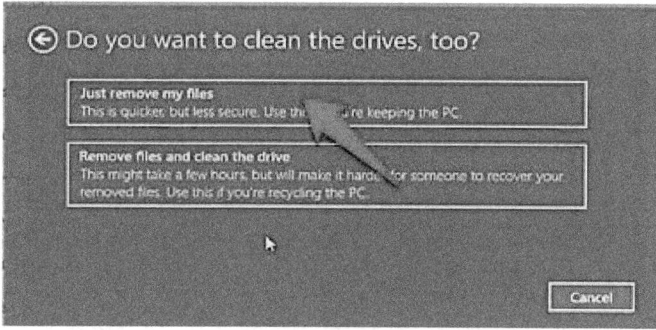

Click on "Reset"

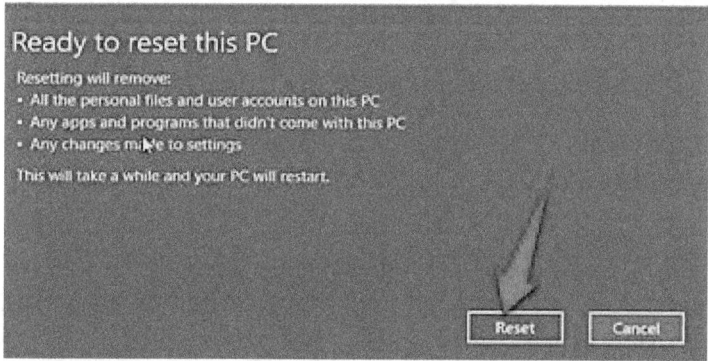

This will take a while to complete. Click "Got it" when the window below pops up

Next, a new Window will be installed. These will take a couple of minutes.

Next, you will need to enter your region, language, keyboard and time zone information.

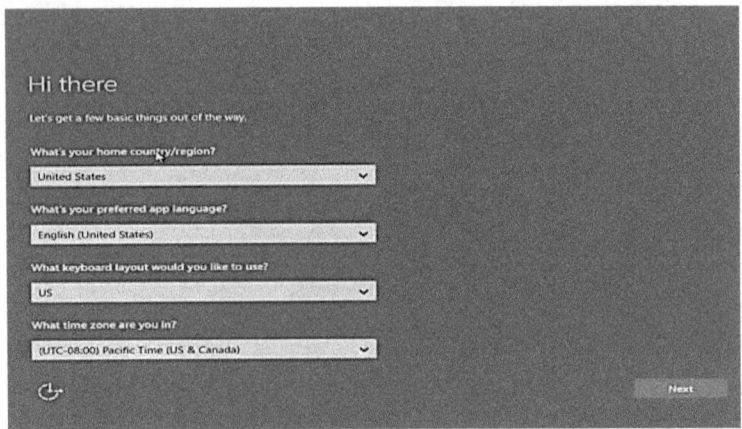

Click "Next" when done - Accept the end user license agreement - "Use Express Settings" to speed up the setup process a little bit - However, you can "customize" your settings when installing Windows 10.

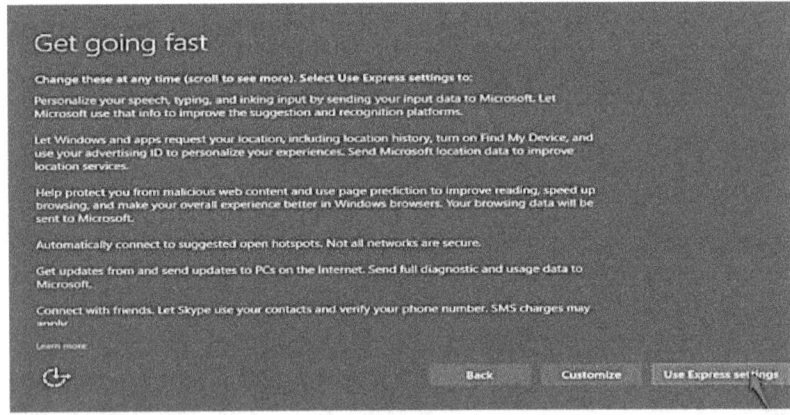

Next, log into your Microsoft account with your email, phone number or Skype and key in your password. If you don't have a Microsoft account, click on the "Create one!" to sign up for one, it's free. You could also skip this step and create a local account in your PC - click on "Skip this step". Choose to enable or skip Cortana. If there is an update waiting, you will be prompted to update your Operating System. Click on "Update or "Not now" to skip the process. You will be logged into a freshly installed Windows.

Speed up Windows 10

The need for a fast PC, especially for gamers, cannot be overemphasized. You will observe that over time, PCs running on the Windows operating systems begins to slow down and in some cases, you might opt to get a replacement. We will look at steps to prevent that crawling windows experience and make you have a more enjoyable time using your PC. All you need to achieve this is to optimize your settings, reduce clutter, clean up and maintain your PC.

If you realize you PC is becoming too slow to perform tasks like gaming and other basic operations, take the following steps outlines below to increase the speed. Type in "Settings" in the search bar - "Click on Privacy Setting" - Under the General tab, turn everything OFF, For Location, turn everything OFF, For Cameras, turn OFF Facebook, Microsoft Edge, OneNote, Store, Maps and Twitter. For the "Microphone" Turn microphone OFF for every app you are not using. For Notification, you can turn it ON or OFF. Ignore "Speech, inking and typing". Leave "Account Info" ON. Turn everything using "Contacts," "Calendar," "Call History,"

"Email," "Messaging," and "Sync with devices" OFF. For Feedback, change "<u>Windows should ask for my feedback</u>" and "<u>Diagnostic and usage data</u>" to NEVER and BASIC respectively. For Background Apps, allowing apps to run at the background will consume resources and also affect your PCs performance, so turn OFF as many apps you don't use at the background. Note that all settings revert to default whenever you install an update, always go back to re-set them. Next is the <u>system setting</u>; in the settings menu, click on "Systems" - Uninstall Apps you don't use under the "Apps & Features," Under the "Offline Map" turn everything OFF. Next step is <u>Power settings</u> - to get to the power settings, hit the start button and in the search bar type in "Power Settings" then click on "Power & Sleep" settings - In the "Power & Sleep" Settings menu, Click on "Additional Power Settings" - Under the preferred plan, select "High Performance."

Next step, "<u>Optimize services</u>" - Click on the start button and in the search bar type "Services." In the "Services" menu is a long list of processes that runs at the background. Be careful not to "stop" just anything here so as not to interfere with the performance of your computer. There are a few things that we will need to stop to increase the speed of your PC. Firstly, disable DMWapppush Service - right click on the service - go to "properties" - change "Startup type" to Disabled then click "Apply". Next, disable all "Xbox live services." Other services you should disable to speed up your PC include AllJoyn Router Service, dmwappushsvc, downloaded Maps Manager,

Diagnostic Tracking Services, Geolocation Service, All Hyper V services, Microsoft Windows SMS Router Service, Remote Access/Desktop Services and Touch Keyboard/ Handwriting Services.

Next, optimize "Personalization." Right-click on the desktop and click on "Personalization" - turn OFF everything under "Start." You should also limit the number of animation by windows to increase your performance. To do this, hit the "Start" button - in the search bar type "System Settings" and click on "View Advanced System Settings."

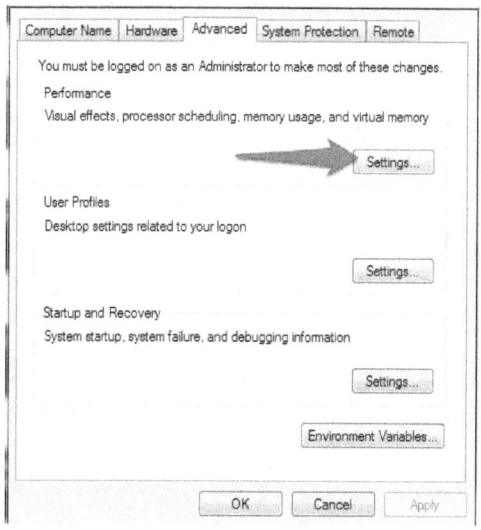

Click on "Advanced" and under "Performance," click "Settings" and Click on "Adjust for best performance." This turns everything OFF.

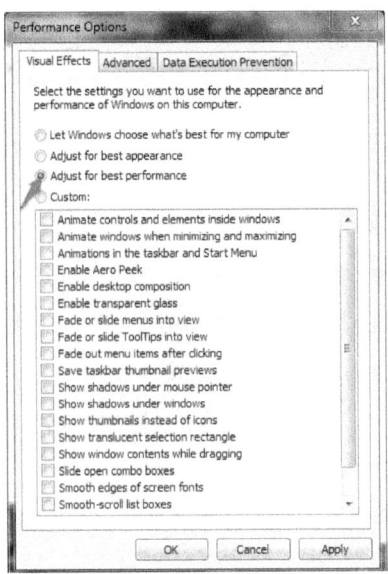

Now, turn ON the following options - Show window contents while dragging, smooth the edges of screen fonts and show thumbnails instead of icons. To reduce clutters, you will need to uninstall any unused programs, browser extensions and background applications.

A Software that can help you do this is the "CCleaner". This is a free software that should be installed on your windows OS to help you get rid of anything you don't need on your PC. After installing the CCleaner - Click on "Tools" - scroll to "Uninstall" and it will display a list of unused programs. Run through the list to check out programs or extension you don't need. Click on the program and Click "Uninstall" at the top-right corner. For browser plugging, scroll to "Browser Plugging" on the CCleaner App and click on the Browser you use often. Run through and select any plugging you don't use anymore. Other features of the CCleaner App are the "Duplicate finder," "System Restore" and "Drive wiper." Next step in the System optimization process is Cleanups/Maintenance - For cleanups, we are talking about physical cleaning. If your system has too much dust, it will heat up components and potentially damaging them. It is ideal to blow your PC often with a dust blower.

Dust blower

Apart from the physical cleaning, there is the digital cleaning you can perform using the CCleaner. There is a tab on the CCleaner called "Cleaner". Click on "Analyze" - this will show you a list of temporary files (e.g. cache) on your computer you don't need - Click on "Run Cleaner" to free up memory. Finally, you would need to defrag your system - on the search bar type "Disk Defragmenter" - and click on Defragment disk. This process rearranges the files for easier access. This also speeds up your computer.

Final Note

Thank you for purchasing this guide and I hope it helps you understand the Windows 10 Operating System and the recent updates. We will try to keep the guide up-to-date as Microsoft rolls out new Windows 10 updates in the future. Please drop feedback by way of reviews to help us improve in our next edition.

Books by the Author

https://www.amazon.com/dp/B07DH7FK3B

https://www.amazon.com/dp/B07L5PRYXX

https://www.amazon.com/dp/B07L5PRYXX

CPSIA information can be obtained
at www.ICGtesting.com
Printed in the USA
BVHW042145250719
554423BV00016B/186/P